Social-Emotional Learning Activities for After-School
and
Summer Programs

Susanna Palomares

Cover: Dave Cowan

ISBN - 10: 1-56499-063-1

ISBN - 13: 978-1-56499-063-1

INNERCHOICE Publishing
15079 Oak Chase Court
Wellington, FL 33414

www.InnerchoicePublishing.com

Contents

Introduction

Successful after-school and summer learning programs provide young people with fun, enriching, challenging experiences in safe and supportive, adult-supervised environments. Mounting evidence indicates that *how* and *where* children and youth spend their out-of-school time has profound effects on their development and safety. This has provoked increasing interest in, and support for, after-school and summer programs.

After-school and summer learning programs offer ideal venues for systematically developing critical life skills. Social-emotional learning (SEL) is based on sound theory and solid research and is designed to encourage positive personal, social, and ethical behavior in children and young people. Through effective SEL instruction, children learn to recognize, understand, and manage their emotions, understand and value others, create and work toward positive goals, make responsible decisions, and successfully manage interpersonal relations. After-school/ summer learning programs provide a less structured and more relaxed environment than the regular classroom, where young people can experience engaging activities like games, role-play, art, music, and creative projects of all types.

With their active, yet focused, approach to skill development, after-school/summer learning programs have a significant role to play in preparing young people for the challenges and opportunities of the 21st century. We look to today's youth to become the knowledgeable, responsible, and empathetic citizens and leaders of tomorrow. After-school/summer learning programs can greatly influence the realization of this future and are without question a worthwhile social investment with the potential for long-term positive impact.

Social -Emotional Learning and Academics

While SEL may seem like the warm, fuzzy side of education, a growing body of research shows that social and emotional competence boosts academic achievement. SEL is not just about better social functioning. It's also about achieving academically. When children possess self-management skills, understand how to get along with others, and build positive relationships, they show improvement on virtually every behavioral measure, including cognitive development and academic performance.

Research also indicates that children with well developed SEL skills are better able to resist the perils of violence and crime, drug and alcohol abuse, depression, anxiety, eating disorders and teen pregnancy.

Social-Emotional skills are crucial to success in school, work and relationships and greatly affect quality of life. Young people who enter adulthood lacking social-emotional skills will be hard pressed to fulfill their potential and find success in personal, professional and civic life.

> *A growing body of literature suggests that a deliberate and comprehensive approach to teaching children social and emotional skills can raise their grades and test scores, bolster their enthusiasm for learning, reduce behavior problems and enhance the brains cognitive functions.*
>
> *Education Week,*

How This Book Will Serve You

The activities in this book are designed to encourage positive interaction among participating children, and between adults and children. Both engaging and challenging, the activities encourage initiative, decision-making, creativity, critical thinking, skill development, and talent sharing. Rather than a hit or miss approach, the book provides a coordinated and sequenced set of skill development activities. Areas of focused skill development include:

- awareness of feelings
- managing emotions
- making wise choices
- identifying positive qualities in self and others
- recognizing personal talents
- appreciating differences
- building a work/achievement ethic
- understanding body language
- sharing family traditions
- managing anger effectively
- taking responsibility
- respecting rules
- setting goals
- learning resistance/refusal skills

For optimal impact, after-school/summer learning programs need to devote sufficient time to activities that focus on social-emotional experiences and allow participating children to be actively involved. New skills are rarely acquired from a single experience. Meaningful learning requires multiple experiences, repeated focus and sufficient time. While this book provides complete directions for meaningful learning to occur, it's up to you to follow through.

The activities in this book are designed to accommodate a wide range of learning styles. Most encourage *active* learning, or learning by doing. Lectures alone rarely produce growth and learning, but when young people get their bodies as well as their brains involved, much progress can be made toward mastery. This is truly a hands-on curriculum.

A Place Where Kids Want to Be

After-school/summer learning programs must compete with a host of alternatives for the time and attention of children. While most of these alternatives have positive appeal, many have a negative impact. But the fact is, competition is real and strong.

The best way to ensure your program's growth and success is to make certain that you provide an enjoyable place for young people to spend their time, that they feel welcome and safe, and that everyone is treated with respect. Too often, leaders confuse what is of interest and fun for children with what is of interest and fun for themselves. To compete successfully takes more than just getting children to participate. It takes creating real value for the children as they see it.

> *All children wear the sign:*
> *I want to be important*
> *NOW! Many of our juvenile*
> *delinquency problems arise*
> *because nobody reads the sign.*
>
> Dan Pursuit

Children like to be in places where they are happy and comfortable. The secret of success is to be such a place. Combining your interest and enthusiasm as a leader with activities and experiences that work for children will help you to create a place where children want to be.

Developing Peer Power

One of the strongest external influences in our lives is peer pressure. When we think of peer pressure, we frequently give it a negative connotation, as in situations where we are forced to do things regardless of whether we want to or not. Yet groups can and do bring pressure to bear on their members—and individuals do bring pressure to bear on other individuals. Peer pressure happens. Because it does, this book offers many activities to help children deal with peer pressure more effectively.

In strengthening your program, however, we hope that you will concentrate on developing *peer power*. Peer power doesn't force children to do things. Rather, it is an encouraging process that provides guidance and support for each child.

Every activity and experience provided in this book delivers a measure of peer power. Children don't simply learn skills, they become aware of the influence they have individually and collectively on friends, associates, and loved ones. From these activities and experiences grow peer power, and from peer power comes strength, vitality, and success for you and your program.

Creating Strength Through Diversity

In our world, we spend a lot of time noticing how we differ from one another. One fact is clear: being different is one thing we all have in common. Everyone is different and everyone is unique. As a leader, you can expect all kinds of children to become involved in your program. Knowing this, one thing is absolutely vital. Your program must make a place for every child who wants to participate.

To help you deal with diversity, here are some ideas to keep in mind:

- Differences are never limited to physical appearance; they involve talents, abilities, beliefs and values, personalities, learning styles, brain orientation and dominance, and behavior, to name a few.
- Just as the children differ from one another, you differ from them.
- The children are aware of differences, including how they view themselves as being different from you.
- To the degree that you make room for these differences in your program, you add depth and value to your efforts.

When we bring together individuals and combine their unique abilities and talents, we gain collective strength. Just as it is important for you as a leader to know the value of differences, it is even more important that the children learn this vital lesson. Respect and appreciation for individual differences forms a basis for shared stewardship and accountability in life and is an important element of social-emotional learning.

It's Up to You!

While this book provides ideas, activities, and directions, you, the program leader or teacher, are the most vital ingredient. Your positive interactions with the children—your love, caring, and concern for each individual child—are the catalysts that will bring depth and meaning to each experience. Cooperative spirit is not something that can be conveyed between the covers of a book. In order for the children to develop habits of self-love, self-care, and an active concern for others, these attributes must first be demonstrated to them. The experiences in this book are like dormant genetic materials—until you bring them to life.

> *People may forget what you say,*
> *People may forget what you do,*
> *But, people never forget the way*
> *you made them feel.*
>
> *Maya Angelou*

Tips for Effective Instruction

Encourage creative and critical thinking. Most of the activities in this book include several discussion questions to ask at the conclusion of the activity. The body of the activity is the affective or emotional component; the discussion questions are the cognitive or critical thinking component. The important thing to remember is that you are not looking for "right" answers. Rather, you want the children to actively think about, process, and learn from the experience in which they have just engaged. Be accepting and encouraging of what the children say, and foster creative thinking.

Allow think-time. When you give directions or ask questions, allow time for mental processing. Typically, teachers allow between 0.7 and 1.4 seconds of silence before continuing to talk or permitting a student to respond—insufficient time for thinking and information processing. Allow at least 3 seconds of silence after each question to give children important cognitive processing time. Count out 3 seconds and notice how it feels. Compare it to the length of time you usually wait. You may be surprised. Remember the brain's need for processing time when you give directions, too. Give one direction at a time and wait 3 seconds.

> *If your emotional abilities aren't in hand, if you don't have self-awareness, if you are not able to manage your distressing emotions, if you can't have empathy and have effective relationships, then no matter how smart you are, you are not going to get very far.*
>
> *Daniel Goleman*
> *Emotional Intelligence*

Build on prior knowledge. People more easily learn and remember new information when they can relate it to something already known. Scientific research into learning and the human brain has established that the only way information can enter the brain is through existing neural networks. In other words, new information must attach itself to a network of existing knowledge. The human brain learns by building on what it already knows. When giving directions, asking questions, or talking with the children, use language and examples with which the children are familiar. When leading the activities in this book, feel free to expand the directions and explanations beyond those provided. You know your children, their backgrounds and experiences. Talk and interact with them to broaden your understanding of "where they are at." Use this knowledge to choose relevant words, examples, directions and questions. Look for what your children already know, understand, and believe, and build your lessons around that knowledge.

Encourage social interaction. This book is chock full of socially engaging experiences for a reason. Humans are social beings, and most learning takes place in a social context. To boost learning, encourage interaction, sharing, and teamwork. Child-to-child relationships matter, as do adult-child relationships. It is through our interconnectedness that we educate children to become fully developed people. Allow the children to share, plan, design, create, problem solve, and relate with one another.

Have fun. Emotions, laughter and just plain fun are all good for learning. Positive, engaging experiences lower stress and increase the availability of neurotransmitters needed by the brain for alertness and memory. The activities in this book, from role-play and music to art, games, movement and dance, are designed to promote learning by engaging the emotional as well as cognitive centers of the brain. By promoting joyful fun, you help the children learn and retain important life skills.

You hold in your hands a tool that will help you provide delightful experiences while purposefully teaching important social-emotional learning skills. Enjoy the experience.

The Beat Goes On

Music and Brainstorming

What this activity teaches:

- Upbeat music can cause us to feel happy.
- Songwriters express feelings and thoughts.
- We are creative!

Materials:

CDs of assorted music of your choice, CD player

Directions:

1. **Introduce the activity by saying to the children:** *Have you ever noticed how powerful music is? It can influence our feelings and moods. To show you what I mean, I brought some songs I want you to hear.*

2. **Listen and discuss:** Play a few of your favorite songs for the children. If possible, choose songs that express different moods. After each song, ask the children what kind of mood the song had and how they liked it. End with a song that is upbeat and happy. Emphasize how much you like the happy song.

3. **Tell the children that they are going to become songwriters. Say:** *Let's write an upbeat song! Something that will make us feel good when we sing it together—or that each of us can sing when we're alone and want to cheer ourselves up. Just humming or singing it will give us good feelings.*

4. Help the children select a tune they all know and like. As a group, brainstorm new words to the song. As the children propose words and phrases, write them down on chart paper for everyone to see. Keep the process upbeat; don't allow the children to criticize one another's ideas. Accept all positive suggestions. If the group gets stuck, share your own ideas. If more than one idea is suggested for the same line, ask the children to vote for the one they like best.

5. When the song is complete, sing it together, giving some of the children solo parts.

Other things to try:

If any of the children play instruments, ask them to play along. If they want to dance, encourage them to do so. If possible, perform the song for other groups.

Choose How You Feel

Drama and Discussion

In this activity, you and the children will act out situations in which the behavior of another person caused you to feel upset. You will also consider and act out alternative methods of responding to each situation in a positive way.

What this activity teaches:

- Experiences that upset us can be looked at in other ways.
- Sometimes upsetting experiences can be our best teachers.
- When someone else is down or upset, we don't have to get upset too.

Directions:

1. **Tell the children about an incident that upset you recently. For example, you might say:** *Today, my neighbor did something that upset me. Let me show you what my neighbor did. I'll play the part of my neighbor. Who wants to be me?*

2. **Initiate the Drama and Discussion and keep it going:** Tell the child who volunteers to be you in your drama, what you said and did in the actual situation. Then act out the scene playing the part of the neighbor.

3. When the drama is over, thank the child who volunteered. Then ask the children: Why do you think my neighbor did that? Help them see that your neighbor was probably just in a bad mood and didn't care how you felt.

4. **Ask:** *Is there anything I could have said or done that might have helped me feel better?* Take suggestions and provide your own suggestions as well. Then act out one or two. Keep it humorous. Laugh with the children.

5. **Invite the children to act out their own dramas. Ask them:** *Has anyone else had something like this happen? Without telling us the name of the person who upset you. Tell us what happened.* Allow children to share their stories. After the children have shared, have them divide up into pairs (or small groups if the drama involved more than two people) and to plan their dramas. Have each pair or group share their drama with the entire group.

Discussion:

After each child's drama, ask the entire group these key discussion questions:

— *Why do you think the other person in this drama acted that way?*
— *Is there anything you could do in this situation to keep from getting upset or to feel better?* Act out one or two positive suggestions.

Explain to the children and help them understand that they have a choice in how they respond to events in their lives, and it's not the event but how they react to it that will determine how they feel.

A Natural High

Art/Poster-Making

What this activity teaches:

- There are lots of easy ways people can make themselves feel good.
- Natural highs are the best highs.

Materials:

Poster paper, crayons, poster paints, magic markers and/or chalk in lots of colors; magazines with ads for ideas.

Directions:

1. Place the materials on a central table or distribute them to individual workstations. Tell the children that they are going to have an opportunity to make some funny posters that suggest ways in which people can cheer themselves up when they are feeling down.

2. **Explain:** *Make your poster look like an ad that tries to get people to buy some sort of drug, or beer, or whatever. You could use words like, "Feeling down? Try this..." only instead of beer or a drug, suggest other things they can do to make themselves perk up, like "smell swell smells," or "taste great tastes." Things that are natural highs and don't cost a dime. Get it? After we finish the posters, we'll make arrangements to put them up where people will see them.*

3. As the children work, give them a few suggestions, but let them create independently. Urge them to make the words and people in their posters extra large so they will show up well. Allow plenty of time for creativity, but be sure to stop the activity early enough for the children to clean up.

4. While they work, talk with the children about the tricky ways in which ads influence people to buy their products. Discuss how natural highs are really the best highs. Ask the children to predict how people will react when they see the posters.

5. When the children have finished their posters, have them share what they have created with the rest of the group. Then display the posters in a prominent place.

Song Lyrics Are Important
Music Activity

What this activity teaches:

- We need to be selective about the music we listen to.
- Music has the power to influence us.
- To feel good about ourselves and about life we can listen to positive, upbeat songs.

You will need:

CD player, CDs of contemporary music, and, if possible, written lyrics to some of the songs (lyrics can be downloaded at www.elyrics.net). Attempt to find songs that include negative messages, as well as songs with a positive message.

Directions

1. **Gather the children together:** Tell them you want them to listen to some music. Ask them to focus on what the words are saying. Play both positive and negative songs.

2. **Explain:** *Because of the music, we don't always pay attention to the words in the lyrics. Sometimes those words have a positive message, and other times they are very negative, giving us messages we might not want.*

3. As the children listen carefully to the lyrics, point out that music is powerful, and that it is important to avoid negative messages, or at least be aware of them. Sometimes the lyrics talk about taking drugs or other unhealthy, illegal, or unacceptable things.

Discussion:

After you have listened to a number of different songs, lead a discussion by asking these and your own questions:

—What do you think the real message is in this song?
—Why is it important to be aware of what songs are saying to us?
—How do negative songs make you feel?
—How do upbeat, positive songs make you feel?

Other things to try:

Have the children listen to songs at home and bring in one CD and the lyrics to one song to share with the group. Remind them that you want them to select a song to share that has a positive message.

Play It Again
Musical Activity/Air Band

What this activity teaches:

- We can select and enjoy music that is positive and that contributes good things to the world.
- Performing with others in a group requires cooperation and planning.

Planning:

Allow parts of two class periods for Air Band (a musical production featuring lip-sync and "instrument-sync" performances to recorded music). One to plan and prepare, and one to perform.

You will need:

CD player to play CDs children bring in for their air bands. An assortment of real or toy instruments, especially drums, and guitars. Objects to serve as microphones, both standing and hand held.

Directions:

1. Place the CD player where it can be heard. Leave a large space for the "bands." Children can sit on the floor or in chairs, if available.

2. Explain: *We are going to create air bands. Choose an individual or a group that you would like to perform to, making sure that the group is singing positive lyrics. BECOME your favorite musical group or singer. Lip sync the words and try to copy the movements of your group as closely as possible. We'll take some time to practice, and then perform for each other.* Work with the children to help them pick songs to perform that have positive words explaining that positive words can be uplifting and make you feel good, and that's what you focus on in this program

3. Have the children form teams. Have each team choose a musical group and song it would like to imitate. Encourage as much "show biz" as possible. The children may want to check at home and/or with neighbors to locate props and costumes.

4. While the children are working on their acts, discuss the fact that many musical groups take a strong pro-social stand on things like the environment, world peace, ending world hunger, etc.. Rap groups and rock stars also sing out against drugs in their songs. Encourage awareness of the positive side of music and song lyrics.

Other things to try:

Invite parents and friends to a performance of the air bands. Make and award Grammies, being sure that everyone wins in some category. Video tape the children as they perform, so they can see themselves later.

Planning a Party

Choice Making and Debrief

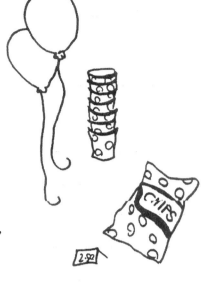

What this activity teaches:

- Making good choices often requires careful thought.
- We can manage on a budget.
- We can say no to some attractive things, while saying yes to others.

Materials:

Paper and pencil for each child, catalogs and flyers displaying an assortment of inexpensive items that would be provided at a party (i.e., candy, cake, cookies, soft drinks, paper plates, napkins, etc.).

Directions:

1. Gather the children together and tell them: *Pretend you are planning a party. You have exactly $50 to spend. You need to figure out what kind of party you can have with $50. To help you do this, we are going to look through these catalogs and flyers I've brought in and choose inexpensive items you would like to provide at your party.* The children will need pencils and paper with which to list the items they think they need, and record the actual cost of items on their papers.

2. As the children work, circulate and help as needed with their choices. Remind them that they need to add the cost up as they go along.

3. Have the children share their lists, plans, and costs for the party they would like to throw.

Discussion:

Lead the children in a discussion about their choices, giving each child a chance to respond to these questions:

- *Did you have enough money in your budget to do all that you wanted to do for your party?*
- *If you didn't have enough money, how did you decide which things you could and could not get?*
- *What did you see that was not on your list that you thought would be excellent for your party?*
- *What kinds of things did you plan with your $50 budget.*

It's About "Me"
Speaking/Collecting Activity

What this activity teaches:

- Identifying and prioritizing things that are important to us can help us become more aware of our values.
- Learning what is important to another person can help us understand that person better.

You will need:

"Me" bags—one per child—containing things that represent the children's interests.

Planning:

Before conducting this activity, ask the children to gather pictures, treasures, and memorabilia that have some meaning to them, place them in a brown paper bag, and bring the bag on a designated day. This is their "Me" bag. Show them an example, by displaying a bag of your own memorabilia.

Directions:

1. Have the children form a circle with their bags in front of them. Ask for volunteers, or draw names to determine the order of sharing.

2. Explain: *Pick items out of your bag, show them, and share with the group what each thing is and why it is important to you. Tell us if it is something you like or dislike, and how you came to have this thing. For example, you might explain that you brought ticket stubs from a special movie or concert you attended. Or you might show a picture of a ballerina because you want to take dance lessons and would like to be a performer someday.*

3. As the children share, some of them may need a little prompting from you. If they are shy or reluctant, ask questions like, *Was that a gift?* or *Would you like to tell us why that is important to you?* Make sure the children take their bags with them when they leave for the day.

Other things to try:

Have the children make collages out of magazine pictures that show likes and dislikes. Make a scrapbook of special things.

The "Inside" and the "Outside" Me

Art/Container Collages

What this activity teaches:

- It is important that we know ourselves, especially our positive qualities and feelings.
- We are learning to more effectively share our positive selves with other people.

You will need:

Any large cans with lids (such as coffee cans) or shoeboxes with lids, magazines, colored paper, yarn, scraps of cloth, crayons or magic markers, scissors, and white glue.

Directions:

1. Place the materials on large tables or at other locations where the children will be working. Give each child a container. The children will glue an assortment of pictures from magazines, pieces of material, yarn, colored paper, and/or their own designs to the outside and inside of their containers.

2. Explain: *We will each decorate a container on the outside and inside to show our positive outer and inner qualities. On the outside, glue pictures, designs, and colored cloth that represent positive personal qualities that you would like to show others. Decorate the inside of the container to show some of the good inner feelings you have about yourself.*

3. As the children work, decorate a container yourself. Suggest that the children use pictures of kids having fun, beautiful colors or designs, and fabrics that seem to represent particular feelings or qualities. Let them be as creative as they wish, as long as their efforts are positive. Allow plenty of time for work and cleanup.

4. During the activity, talk to the kids about positive qualities and feelings and the kinds of pictures and designs that can be used to represent them. Ask the children to talk about their choices, acknowledging each child with appreciation.

5. Conclude the activity by conducting a sharing session during which the children show their decorated containers and talk about their inner and outer qualities. Remind the children to be honest and sincere about their feelings. As the children share, do not allow any put downs or joking at others' expense. Let the children take their containers home to use as storage for some of their favorite photos, letters, or other treasures.

Stand Up! ...Sit Down!

Game

What this activity teaches:

- Each of us is a unique person with specific, identifiable characteristics.
- We are alike and different in many ways.

You will need:

A lot of children (20 or more works best), chairs for all but one child.

Directions:

1. This game is similar to musical chairs. Place the chairs in a large circle, facing inward. Direct all of the children to sit in a chair. One child will be left over. Have that child stand in the center of the circle.

2. Explain: *In this game, the child in the middle will say, "I like my neighbor who..." and then name some characteristic that describes any person in the circle. For example, the child may add, "is wearing a T-shirt," "has a dog," "is less than 10 years old," or "has brown eyes." The characteristic does not have to describe the person who is "It," but it must be positive and not embarrassing. As soon as the child names the characteristic, the children who are sitting down who have that characteristic must get out of their chairs and find new chairs. At the same time, the child in the middle must try to scramble for one of the empty chairs. Whoever is left without a chair is then "It."*

3. Before starting the game, stress the ground rule: No Running or Pushing. If the children feel like running, they must do it in slow motion. Demonstrate slow motion running, exaggerating your slow movements. The kids will imitate you and safely have fun.

4. Something to think about: Almost all people like to be in the spotlight, even if they won't admit it. So allow the game to proceed until each child has been in the spotlight at least once.

Another game to play:

"Because I Live..." is a verbal game in which the children take turns telling the group about ways in which they have contributed to their world. Sitting in the circle, they complete the sentence, "Because I live...," adding phrases such as "my dad has someone to help him with the dishes," "Bill has a best friend," "my little sister has someone who reads to her," or " the lawn gets mowed every week."

Making It Better

Art/Construction

What this activity teaches:

- We improve our skills (and lives) through effort and experience.
- Things that seem difficult to do at first, usually get easier as we practice doing them.

You will need:

Sheets of paper, (approximately 6 sheets per participant), scissors, magic markers, glue, old magazines (from which to cut decorations), paper clips, measuring tape (25 ft. or longer), and paper and pencil for recording distances.

Directions:

1. Gather the children together and tell them: *Today we will all have a chance to create a series of paper airplanes and see how far we can fly them. We will try to make each paper airplane better than the last. After you have made a paper airplane, take it to the flight area and fly it a few times to see how far it will go. Measure the longest distance it flew, and then go back to the construction area and build another plane. Try to make changes in the design of the new plane that will make it fly even farther than the first one did. You may decorate your planes to make them uniquely yours. Keep creating and flying planes until I call time.*

2. As the children work, keep your help and suggestions to a minimum, but be supportive and encouraging. Provide enough direction so they know what to do, but allow the children to be the creators. Reinforce the idea that the children are competing with themselves (to improve their planes), not with each other. If possible, set up the flight area outside, in a gym, or in a hallway to maximize flying distance.

Discussion:

After everyone has had a chance to make and fly a number of planes, gather the group together again. Ask them to talk about the experience. Ask the following questions:

> — *Did experience help you improve your plane? How?*
> — *Is improving yourself like improving the paper airplanes? How?*
> — *How is improving our airplane design so it flies better like improvements people might want to make in their lives?*

Design for Building the Paper Airplanes

1. Carefully fold an 8-1/2 x 11 inch piece of paper lengthwise to make a crease in the paper—

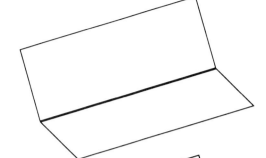

2. Fold the two lead corners back along the original crease to form a point..

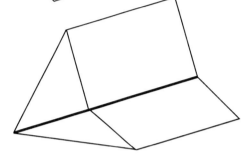

3. Fold the pointed end back to about 1" from the end of the paper and in line with the crease.

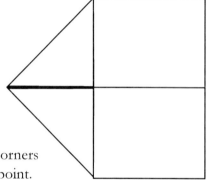

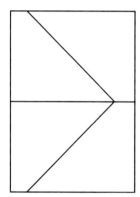

4. Now, just as in step 2., fold the lead corners back along the crease to form a new point.

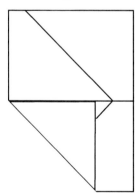

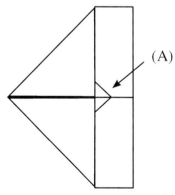

(A)

5. Fold the small tab (A) toward the pointed end. This locks in the previous folds and sets up the creations of the wings.

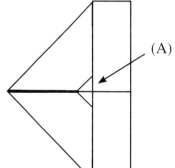

(A)

6. Fold along the crease as shown.

7. Now you're ready to make the wings. To do this fold each wing from the point so that the leading edge of the wing folds down to the original crease as shown below.

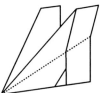

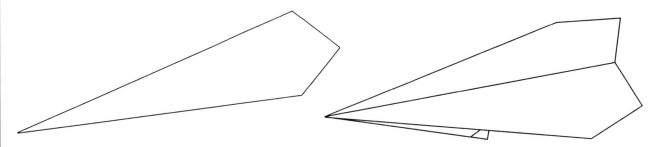

YOU ARE NOW READY TO FLY!
(BUT THERE IS MORE)

8. Since the wings tend to separate when the dart is released you can improve performance by placing a piece of tape across the back of the plane as shown below to secure the wings together.

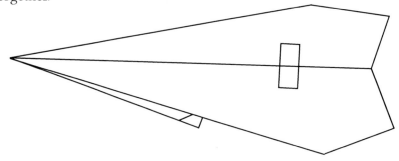

Try launching the airplane first without the tape and then with the tape to see the difference. Also try other things like bending the trailing edges of the wings up and down. You may even want to attach a paper clip at various places on the body of the dart to see what influence weight has on its flight.

Place a 25-foot tape measure on the floor or ground and see what design changes give the longest flight. Above all have fun!!

Creating Unique Creatures

Art/Creative Expression

What this activity teaches:

- Each of us has special qualities, like fingerprints and toeprints, that make us unique.
- The things we create can be just as unique as our fingerprints and toeprints.

You will need:

Large sheets of paper, magic markers, crayons, and other available art materials.

Directions:

1. Provide each child with a large sheet of paper and put out the art materials.

2. Explain: *We are going to make outlines of our hands and feet and use them to create a unique creature. First, use the magic markers to trace each hand and then each foot (without your shoes) on your large piece of paper. The tracings can face any direction and be in any position. Next, using the art materials, make a creature out of your hand and feet outlines. Add a body and head and connect all the parts in some way.* Suggest that they use a variety of colors, directions, and patterns to make their creatures unique.

3. While they make their creatures, discuss the fact that, just as no two snowflakes are exactly alike, no two people in all the world have fingerprints or toeprints exactly alike. That makes each of use unique. Talk about other qualities that make people unique and special.

4. After the creatures are completed, display them on the walls for everyone to see. Suggest that the children take them home at the end of the day or week.

My Name In a Poem

Acrostic Poetry-Writing

What this activity teaches:

- We can think and write good things about ourselves.
- Thinking and saying something good about ourselves can help us to feel good.

You will need:

Sheets of newsprint or poster paper, crayons, magic markers, or colored chalk.

Preparation:

Acrostic poems are poems or writings that are built on the letters of a word, or a name. For example, if your name were George, you might create an acrostic poem about yourself, like this:

Generous to a fault
Enthusiastic in everything I do
Orderly, but not picky
Real as I can be
Guarded at times
Eager to please

Before the session, write a sample acrostic poem to show the children. Use your name or a word that describes you as the basis for the poem.

Directions:

1. Gather the children together and tell them: Today, we are going to write "acrostic" poems. In this kind of poem, each line begins with a letter from a name or word. Here is an example I made using the letters of my own name. First I wrote my name down the left edge of the paper. Then I wrote positive statements about myself across the paper. Each statement had to start with one of the letters of my name. Use your name and then write a word or statement beginning with each letter of your name that describes one of your positive qualities—like brilliant, great, or radical. Make your letters large so they can be seen easily, and use as much of the paper as possible.

2. As the children work, give them help and suggestions as needed, but don't do the work for them. Emphasize that the lines they write should make positive statements about themselves.

Discussion:

After everyone has had time to complete an acrostic poem, ask the children to share and discuss what they have done. Suggest that they take their poems home and put them up—as reminders of their positive qualities.

Other things to try:

Use this as a small group activity. Break the children into groups of 3 or 4 and have each group choose a word and turn it into an acrostic poem. Or assign a fun word to each group.

Who Am I?

Drama/Role-Playing

What this activity teaches:

- We all have people we admire and wish we could be like.
- The strengths we admire in others are often the strengths we would like to develop in ourselves.

You will need:

Room enough for the children to sit in a circle or a semi-circle while each of them performs. Costume-making materials and equipment (optional).

Directions:

1. Gather the children together and tell them: *Today, each of you is going to have the opportunity to role play (act out) a person you admire. The person you choose could be a sports figure, or a TV, movie, or rock star. Or you could choose an occupation, such as astronaut, crime fighter, or teacher. Before you begin role-playing, tell us if you are acting out a real person or an occupation, but don't tell us who or what it is. The rest of us are going to ask questions and try to guess the person or occupation you are acting out.*

2. If any of the children has trouble thinking of someone to role play, ask questions that will lead that child to make a choice. If costume-making materials are available, suggest how the children might use them.

Discussion:

After each child acts out a favorite person or occupation, ask some of the following questions:

— *What is it that you admire about this person or occupation?*
— *What special strengths or abilities does this person (people in this occupation) have?*
— *Do you have any of those strengths or abilities yourself? Which ones?*

Puppets – Part I

Art/Puppet Making

Note:

This two-part puppet activity has a different focus depending on the ages of the children with whom you are working. For younger children the puppets can be described as "a new friend" they are creating. Then, the puppet plays are enacted for the benefit of the group.

Older children can be told that they will be creating puppets to put on puppet plays for younger children.

What this activity teaches:

- Creating something can be fun.
- Things we create express our thoughts, likes, and feelings.

You will need:

Styrofoam or plain paper cups, material scraps, magic markers, and "tacky" glue. An assortment of decorative items, such as buttons, beads, sequins, ric-rak, and yarn (some of which may be brought by the children).

Directions:

1. Place the materials on a table or workspace. Tell the children that they are going to create cup puppets. The cups will become the heads of the puppets, and the children will decorate them with the materials.

2. Explain: *We will make the puppet's head by turning the cup upside down and decorating it with the other materials. You can make a boy or a girl puppet, and name it when you are finished. Use a piece of material as "clothing." Glue it on the underside of the cup so that it will hide your hand when you hold the puppet.*

3. While the children work, give them some ideas for decorating their puppets. Suggest that they use yarn for hair, buttons or sequins for eyes, or magic markers to make lips. Encourage their creativity. After the puppets are finished, make sure that everyone helps with clean-up. Then have the children put their puppet heads over their first two fingers, with the material covering their wrists, and have them "talk" to each other.

Other things to try:

As a variation, make sock puppets, paper bag puppets, or stick puppets (from tongue depressors). Decorate them with similar kinds of materials.

Putting On a Puppet Show – Part II

Role-Playing with Puppets

What this activity teaches:

- We can use puppets to communicate our thoughts and feelings safely.
- Role-playing can be a rehearsal for real-life situations.
- Practicing positive responses can help prepare us for real-life challenges

You will need:

Puppets made by the children, optional puppet stage (made from a large cardboard box or a table turned on its side).

Directions:

1. Tell the children that their puppets are going "on stage" to respond to questions and situations that are given to them. They will perform in pairs. Younger children will put on the plays in their groups. Allow older children to perform for a group of younger children.

2. Explain: *You can let your puppet act out situations and answer questions by moving it across the stage or shaking its head up and down while it talks. We will take turns putting our puppets on stage. First, have your puppet introduce itself. Next, I will ask a question or present a situation to act out. Your puppet will do the acting and talking.*

3. Begin by dividing the children into teams of two. As each team goes up on stage, lead one or two situations from the list on the following page. Each situation has two characters. Help the children understand the two parts and then decide who will play each part. Have them act out the situation as stated and then work on a positive resolution for each.

4. Allow the older children to practice their puppet plays before presenting them to the younger children. Coach them in acting out positive responses, but let them come up with their own solutions.

Other things to try:

Tell the children to sit in two's, facing each other, and have their puppets respond to each other's questions, rather than go on stage.

Kindness Situations

- You see the new kid in school playing alone, so you go over and talk with him or her.

- Your friend was absent from school today, so you call him or her on the phone to see if everything is okay.

- Your mom needs to go to a meeting and is hurrying to wash the dishes, so you offer to finish the job so that she can leave on time.

- The kid sitting next to you in the lunch room forgot his or her lunch, so you offer to share yours.

- Your next-door neighbor is sick with the flu, so you made a get-well card and brought it over to him or her.

- A new kid in class is from another country and doesn't speak much English. You see that she or he doesn't understand a game the rest of the kids are playing, so you go over to help him or her out.

Problem-Solving Situations

- You've been waiting patiently in a long line when someone cuts in line ahead of you.

- The school bully calls you names.

- You let a friend borrow your favorite toy. You want it back, but now your friend wants to take the toy when he or she goes on vacation.

- Your friend wants to watch a violent movie and you don't want to see it.

- You know the school rule is no running in the halls. No one is around and your friend is running and laughing and telling you to catch up and do the same thing.

- You're washing out some plastic containers to throw away in the recycle bin when a kid comes by and says you're a nerd for doing that.

Communication Without Words

Pantomime and Discussion

What this activity teaches:

- Bodies and facial expressions broadcast feelings.
- Drama is exciting because it portrays emotion.
- We communicate feelings through our body language and facial expressions.

You will need:

Descriptions of situations from the following page written on small pieces of paper, folded and placed in a container—one description for every two children.

Directions:

1. Ask the children to pair up. Have each pair draw one sheet of paper with a situation written on it. Direct each pair to go off to a private place for five minutes and plan a short pantomime of its situation. Explain that the children are to act only with their faces and bodies. They may neither say words, nor make vocal noises. The object is to do such a good job of acting that the group will be able to tell how each actor is feeling in his or her role. If the group can guess the situation, that's fine, but it is not necessary.

2. When the children have finished planning, have them enact their pantomimes one pair at a time. Enjoy each pantomime and clap when it is over.

3. After each pantomime, ask the group to tell the actors how they appeared to be feeling in their roles. Finally, ask the actors to tell the group what the situation was they were acting out.

Discussion:

Ask the children:

- *Do our bodies and faces have a language of their own?*
- *What did you learn about that language through this activity?*
- *Is it important to be aware of what our bodies and faces are "saying" to others?*

Situations for Communication Without Words

- You just got a new puppy and your friend is very jealous.

- You and your friend are walking down a dark street at night. You hear a strange noise, but your friend doesn't hear it. She thinks you're making it up.

- You have the lead role in the school play. You lost track of time and showed up for rehearsal when it was almost over. The director is very upset.

- You have worked very hard on the end-of-the-year class party. Your friend's assignment was to bring the cake. He or she comes to the party empty handed because he or she forgot it was the day of the party.

- It's your birthday and your mother just gave you the thing you wanted most—a new bike.

- Without asking, your sister (or brother) wore your favorite sweater and returned it to you with a rip in the sleeve.

- You and your friend have had a fight. Now you are trying to work things out, but your friend is trying to ignore you.

The Color of Feelings

Discussion and Art

What this activity teaches:

- There are many different kinds of feelings, and they can be created by many different kinds of situations.
- We can express our feelings through art.
- It's important to know how to express our feelings in positive ways.

You will need:

Chart pad, magic markers, white construction paper, crayons or paints.

Directions:

1. Have the children name all the words they can think of that describe feelings. Write them on the chart paper. Make sure that you have at least one word per child. If need be, add to the list yourself. Don't forget words like surprised, confused, delighted, annoyed, frustrated, joyful, ecstatic, depressed, etc. Discuss several possible situations that can cause each feeling.

2. As a group, have the children assign three colors to each feeling word. Take a vote to get a majority opinion. For example, blue, gray, and green may be selected for the word sad; yellow, pink, and orange may represent joyful. Write the three chosen color words next to each feeling word on the board or butcher paper. Don't duplicate any color combination.

3. Tell the children to choose one of the feeling words to illustrate.

4. Distribute construction paper and crayons or paints. Have the children make pictures or create designs that express the feeling words they chose. Tell them to use only the three colors that the group decided would represent that feeling. Allow plenty of time for thinking and creating, but save time for clean-up.

5. As the children work, continue to talk about the different feelings and what might cause them.

Other things to try:

Invite a storyteller to visit the group and tell a story that focuses on feelings (most librarians are good storytellers), or ask the librarian to recommend a book you can read to your group that deals with feelings.

Our Faces Show Feelings

Art/Cartooning

What this activity teaches:

- A person's feelings register on his or her face.
- Different feelings produce different facial expressions.
- We communicate our feelings through our facial expressions.

You will need:

Chart paper, magic markers, pencils with erasers, and bottle lids.

Directions:

1. Tell the children that, after a short demonstration, they will have a chance to draw some cartoons showing how people are feeling.

2. Place a large lid on the chart paper and draw around it with a dark magic marker to produce a circle. Then ask the children to suggest how the features of this cartoon character's face (the circle) could be drawn to show that this cartoon person is scared. Follow their suggestions, perhaps doing several faces, until the cartoon person does look scared. Then, for fun, draw a bubble to show that the cartoon person is saying something, and ask the group what they think you should write there. Write in the idea you all like best.

3. After you have drawn a scared cartoon character, ask the group to help you draw one who is happy, then one who is confused, sad, or embarrassed, etc. Finally, ask the children, *How would you like to give this a try?* You may work by yourself or with a partner. Distribute the materials to the children.

4. While they work, talk with the children about how our faces move and contort to show feelings. Pose for them and urge them to pose for each other. Laugh with the children and have a good time.

Other things to try:

Give the children pastel magic markers with which to add colors to their cartoons. (Pastels won't obscure the original drawings or captions.) Make a book out of the children's finished products.

Sculpt a Feeling
Living Sculptures

What this activity teaches:

- Feeling words mean different things to different people.
- Feelings can be (and usually are) expressed nonverbally, as well as verbally.

You will need:

A small sheet of paper and pencil for each child

Directions:

1. Pass out the paper and pencils to each child. Ask the children to think of four feelings that they've experienced today, and to write them down in the form of feeling words on their sheets of paper. Help the children identify their feelings. When they are through writing, have them fold the papers over to hide the writing. Then tell them to choose partners.

2. Explain that each pair is to pick one person in their pair to be Person A. The other will be Person B. Give the children a moment to accomplish this.

3. Now tell Person A to whisper one of his or her feeling words into Person B's ear. Have all the pairs do this at once.

4. Explain that Person B's job is now to "sculpt" Person A to look as if she or he is experiencing that feeling. Demonstrate by sculpting one of the children to look worried (or some other feeling). Don't tell the children the feeling you are trying to capture. Show them: Put the child's hands together and direct him/her to "wring" them. Gently push the child's eyebrows up in the center to form worry lines. Round the child's shoulders and cause them to shake just a bit. Ask the group to guess what feeling your "sculpture" depicts.

5. After Person B has finished sculpting Person A, have each pair join another pair to form groups of four. Tell them to guess what feeling each other's sculpture represents.

6. Tell the partners to switch roles. Person B now whispers a feeling word to Person A and the activity is repeated. Continue switching roles after each round until all eight feelings (four per partner) have been sculpted.

Discussion:

Get the children to talk about the experience, by asking:

— *When you were the <u>sculptor</u>, how did you decide what to do?*
— *When you were the <u>sculpture</u>, did your partner succeed in making you look like you were feeling?*
— *What did you learn from this activity?*

Family Traditions

Art/Verse

What this activity teaches:

- All families have things they share in common as well as traditions that make them special and unique.
- It is fun and interesting to learn about the families and traditions of other people.

You will need:

Fairly good size pieces of art paper, construction paper, paints, crayons, magic markers, and other art materials.

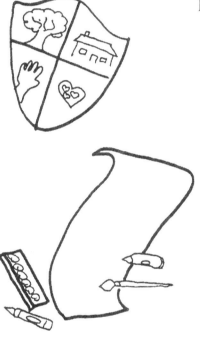

Directions:

1. Gather the children together and tell them: *Today we are going to have a chance to share, through art and verse, some of the things that make our families unique and special. You can do this in a number of ways. You will paint or draw a poster depicting your family traditions. Your poster may show special foods your family likes to eat, clothing family members wear on certain occasions, or activities they take part in on holidays or at other times. You might want to show your different family members and any pets you have. You may also write a verse or story about your family—with or without art work. When you are finished, you will have a chance to share you art or verse with the group."*

2. Give help and suggestions as needed. Assist those who are having difficulty by asking questions such as, *What are some special things your family does at holidays or for celebrations? What is your favorite meal that your family eats together? What is special or different about your family that you are proud of?*

Discussion:

When the children are finished working, gather them together and have them show their art work or read their verse to the group. Then ask:

— *What similarities in our families were depicted in the art and verse we created? What differences?*
— *Why is it good to understand the families and traditions of other people?*

Interviewing Our Families

Communication

What this activity teaches:

- It is fun and interesting to learn about our families and relatives.
- If we ask (and listen) we may learn that older people have had experiences similar to our own.

Directions:

1. A week or so before this activity, give the group the following instructions: *Sometime during this week, I would like you to interview a family member. In the interview, you will ask the person certain questions and write down his or her answers. You may interview a parent, a grandparent, an aunt, or an uncle. If there is no family member available, you may interview an older friend or neighbor.* Provide the children with the following list of questions:

   — *What is the most interesting thing that has happened in your life?*
   — *What was life like when you were my age?*
   — *Who were some of my older relatives? What were they like and what did they do for a living? Where did they live?*
   — *Do you know any interesting stories about them?*

2. After the interviews have been completed, gather the children together and have them share the results of their interviews. Have them read both their questions and the responses of theperson interviewed.

Discussion:

After all of the children have shared their interviews, ask the group the following questions:

— *What did you enjoy most about interviewing a relative or friend?*
— *Did you learn anything new about the person you interviewed?*
— *Did the person you interviewed describe an experience or feeling that you have had too?*
— *Did you learn anything from listening to the interviews that helps you better understand the families of other people?*

Everyone Has Talents
Sharing and Demonstrations

What this activity teaches:

- We all have talents and special aptitudes.
- It's important to share our talents with others.
- We can enjoy and appreciate one another's special abilities.

You will need:

Trophies, photos, or memorabilia brought by the children from home. Camera (optional).

Directions:

1. Preparation: A few days prior to implementing this activity, tell the children that an upcoming session will be devoted to sharing talents and special aptitudes. Ask them to begin thinking about what they can share with the group. Tell them that they will each have an opportunity to talk about their talent, do a short demonstration or performance, or share an object that illustrates their talent.

2. Explain: *Most of us don't get enough opportunities to tell others about the things we do well. We're taught that it's not polite to talk about our talents and achievements too much, so we don't do it at all. Let's forget about that for one day. If you can, bring something to show the group that illustrates your talent. It could be a trophy, a musical instrument, a piece of artwork, or a photograph showing you doing whatever it is you do well. If you like, you can give us a short demonstration of your talent—or you can just tell us about it. The type of talent you have doesn't matter. On this day, all talents and abilities are worth bragging about.*

3. During the activity, have each child in turn share his or her talent or ability. Applaud, and—if you have a camera—take a picture of the child in action.

Something to think about:

Help every child think of something she or he is good at—even if it's taking care of a younger sibling, or doing math problems. Show equal appreciation for all.

Other things to try:

If you take photographs, make a display, including captions for each photo. Or put the photos in a special album and have it available for the children to look at.

Designing Ideal Creatures

Brainstorming and Discussion

What this activity teaches:

- Our imaginations are powerful.
- Though not ideal, humans have many excellent features.
- There are things we can do to make our bodies the best that they can be.

You will need:

A copy of the experience sheets entitled, *Create an Ideal Creature,* for each child; several sheets of chart paper; magic markers in different colors.

Directions:

1. Preparation: Hand out the Experience Sheet *Create an Ideal Creature,* and tell the children that they are going to have a chance to invent creatures that can do everything that they think an ideal creature should be able to do. To make sure they understand the idea, get them to talk a little bit about some of the attributes an ideal creature might have. Allow ample time for the children to finish the Experience Sheets.

2. Ask the children to share their Ideal Creatures with the group. List creature attributes on chart paper, putting a check mark next to an attribute every time it is repeated by a different child. Talk about the advantages of the attributes. Act out some and have a good time.

3. On another sheet of chart paper, help the children create a composite drawing containing all of the favorite features mentioned. Have the children take turns adding features to the drawing, using different colors—or do the drawing yourself, following their directions.

4. Now take each feature in turn, and talk about how it relates to humans. Ask if there's any way the human body could be redesigned to have that feature, or if there's anything a person could do to enjoy the advantages of the feature without really having it. For example, humans aren't disease-free, but when they take good care of themselves, they don't get sick as often.

Discussion:

Ask the children these and other questions:

— *What similarities are there between our Ideal Creature and humans?*
— *Is there such a thing as an ideal human being? What would such a person be like?*
— *If you take care of your body and make it the best that it can be, is that ideal? How can you do that?*

Create an Ideal Creature

Experience Sheet

Have you ever wished you could fly next to a seagull or swim with a dolphin?

Have you ever wanted to have arms come out of your waist when it's your turn to bat?

Have you ever wished you could send up a set of periscope eyes to see over a crowd?

Think about things that you would like to do better. Then think about special things that animals can do.

Now, create an IDEAL CREATURE that has all the best features you can imagine.

List the features here. | List the advantages of the features here.

_____ | _____
_____ | _____
_____ | _____
_____ | _____
_____ | _____
_____ | _____

Draw a picture of your IDEAL CREATURE here:

Give your creature a name.

_____

Making Treasures Out of Junk

An Inventor's Workshop

What this activity teaches:

- It's fun to be creative.
- Inventing involves seeing things in new ways.
- We can all be creative and inventive.

You will need:

A large assortment of "junk:" Bottle caps, screws, bolts, other mechanical parts, hangers, scraps of paper, fabric, and wood, old keys, discarded jewelry, boxes, etc. White glue, scissors, magic markers, and several types of connectors, like wire, string, and paper clips. (If you like, ask each child to bring a small sack of junk from home.) An invention of your own to show as an example.

Directions:

1. Tell the children that they are going to turn junk into creative inventions that have real or imagined functions.

2. Place the materials on a large table, or distribute them among individual workstations. You can have the children work as individuals or in small groups.

3. Explain: *Today we are all inventors. We are going to create unique products out of junk. Let the materials suggest things to you. Take some things and move them around in front of you. Put them together in various ways. What do you see? A robot? A pet groomer? A space station? Can you make a wire hanger into an airplane? Or a plunger into an alien wall-climber? You can make a device, a vehicle, a game, a tool, or just about anything else, as long as you can explain to us what it does. If your invention doesn't really work, that's fine, as long as you can describe to us how it is supposed to work.* Show the children your own invention.

4. As the children work, suggest ways that they can be more inventive—by reversing, combining, rearranging, thinking of opposites, etc. If necessary, help them figure out ways to connect objects together, using glue, wire, etc. Allow time for clean up.

5. Have each child show his or her invention to the group, explaining its function and how it works.

Discussion:

After the sharing, talk about the invention process. Ask the children:

- *What did you like best about this activity?*
- *What thoughts sparked your invention? Where did the idea come from?*
- *How can we be more creative in our everyday activities?*

Getting to the Other Side
Creative Movement

What this activity teaches:

- Our bodies can move in many different ways.
- There are limits to what our bodies can do.
- We can think quickly, and act cooperatively and creatively.

You will need:

A large, empty floor space or grassy area on which to do the activity. CD player and CDs of lively "traveling" music. A large number of children—twenty or more.

Directions:

1. This is an energizing activity that requires quick decisions and encourages children to use their bodies in creative ways. Be prepared for lots of laughter, cheering, and enthusiasm.

2. Have the children find partners and line up at one end of the floor space or grassy area. Tell them: *The object of the activity is to get from one side of this space to the other using a creative movement that no one else has used. You and your partner may either create a single, cooperative movement, or you may do the same movement. If you both do the same movement, you must mirror each other. You may roll, crawl, hop, skip, etc. It's OK to hold hands or link in some other way, but you don't have to.*

3. Point out that the children must watch carefully to see what all other pairs do, so that they don't repeat any movement. Pairs should be planning their traveling movements while they are waiting, because when they reach the head of the line, they must be ready to go as soon as the pair in front of them reaches the other side.

4. It is the responsibility of everyone to stop any pair that repeats a movement that has already been done, and send that pair to the back of the line.

5. Start the music, and begin the activity. If you like, when everyone succeeds in getting to the other side, surprise the children by reversing directions and having them return to the original side—still without repeating any movements.

Other things to try:

Make it a rule that each pair has to link up somehow to create a single cooperative movement. For example, back-to-back with arms linked and hopping only on the two right feet.

Good Things I Do for Myself

Pair Share

What this activity teaches:

- We can become more aware of our physical selves by sharing.
- We take care of our bodies in many different ways.

You will need:

Enough chairs for all of the children, placed in pairs, facing each other, to form a large circle. Chart paper and magic marker. Stop watch or watch with second hand.

Directions:

1. Write the following topics on chart paper and place the chart where it can be seen by all of the children.
    - *Something I Like to Eat That's Good For Me*
    - *My Favorite Sport or Exercise*
    - *How I Take Care of Myself When I'm Sick*
    - *The Best Thing About Me Physically*

2. Have all of the children find a chair. If the chairs are arranged properly, each child will be facing a partner, in a large circle. If one child is left over, you be that child's partner.

3. Explain: *You and your partner are going to take turns talking to each other about one of these topics. When it is your turn to talk, you will have 2 minutes to share. At the end of 2 minutes, I will tell you to switch. Then your partner will share. When you are the listener, listen carefully and don't interrupt. You will have one minute at the end of each round to ask each other questions. When both of you have had a turn, I will ask the outside people to get up and move to their right. Then you will all have new partners for the next topic.*

4. Before starting, ask if anyone has a question about any of the topics. Elaborate briefly, as needed. Start the activity. Allow a total of 5 minutes on each topic, and then have the children change partners.

Discussion:

When the children have finished sharing on all four topics, gather them together and ask:

— *What are some of the good things other people in the group like to eat?*
— *What are some of their favorite sports or exercises?*

A Positive Response to Anger

Art/Verse

What this activity teaches:

- There are positive ways to respond to anger.
- We have the power to change our feelings.

You will need:

A CD or tape of relaxing instrumental music. (optional)

Directions:

1. If you have music, start the tape at a low volume so you can speak over it easily. Make your voice loud enough to be heard, but soft enough to be relaxing. Read the following passage slowly, pausing when you see two dots (...) so the children have ample time to picture things in their minds as you read.

2. Explain: *You are going to take an imaginary trip. Sit in a comfortable position with your eyes closed so that you can imagine things as I talk to you. Make sure you are not touching your neighbor. Now we're ready. Uncross you arms and legs, close your eyes, and take a deep breath. Slowly let it out like this. (Demonstrate this.) Now you do it. Breathe in and let it out. Again. (Continue to breathe in and out with them three to five times.) As you relax . . and take in one more full, deep breath . . and exhale . . excellent . . relax . . Allow your imagination to help you recall a time you were angry. . It may have occurred recently or a long time ago . . a time when you were angry and upset . . Put yourself in that moment . .What do you see?. .What do you hear?. . Can you remember what you said?. . What was it?. . Is there shouting?. . or silence?. . What did you do?. . Did you hit? run?. . break something?. . say things you wish you hadn't?. . Now think of how you wish you had acted . . Could you hit a pillow instead of someone?. . or talk to a friend?. . or write your feelings out?. . exercise?. . Picture the perfect way for you to react to this situation . .What can you say?. . What can you do differently than before?. . See yourself saying exactly the right thing at the right time . . Tell yourself, "I have wonderful self-control" . . "I know many positive ways to handle anger" . . good . . And now, as you gradually shift back to the present moment, allow those positive feelings and ideas to stay with you . . You can call upon these skills any time you choose . . Notice that your breathing is becoming stronger as you gently open your eyes, feeling perfect in every way.*

3. If you're using music, keep it playing. The children may want to stretch.

Discussion:

Ask if anyone would like to share how she or he turned anger into a positive action. Thank those who choose to share. If no one shares, simply tell the children that the imagining technique will work for them anytime.

Actions Speak Louder Than Words

Brainstorming and Pantomime

What this activity teaches:

- Expressions and body language "speak" louder than words.
- There are many levels of angry feelings.

You will need:

Chart paper and magic markers, slips of paper, and a box, jar, or other container to hold the slips of paper.

Directions:

1. Gather the children together and ask: *Have you ever heard someone say, "I'm fine," and known that he or she was mad or sad or something other than "fine?" Our bodies and facial expressions almost always reveal what we are feeling, even if it's not the same as what we are saying.*

2. Brainstorm: Ask the children to name as many words as they can that mean some level of angry. From low levels of angry, like *irritate* and *annoy*, all the way up to high levels like, *furious* and *enraged*. Record their list on chart paper. Leave the chart in place while you copy the words on slips of paper. Place the slips in a container. Have each child draw one slip of paper and pantomime the word. The children can use facial expressions, gestures, and body language, but may say any words. Have the group guess which word (from the chart) is being acted out. Whoever guesses correctly gets to be the next person to draw a word and act it out.

Other things to try:

The children can do a similar activity with partners. One child acts out one of the anger words and the partner pantomimes a positive emotion or feeling. With this variation, a list of positive words would need to be brainstormed along with the anger words. Pairs of words (one from each list) would be placed in the container.

Scary Dreams

Art Activity

What this activity teaches:

- We are powerful.
- We can change scary situations.
- We are in control.

You will need:

Paper, crayons, magic markers, and/or chalk in lots of colors.

Directions:

1. Distribute the materials. Tell the children that they will have a chance to draw something that scares them and then get rid of the thing that scares them in a second drawing.

2. Explain: *We've all had bad dreams or nightmares. Think of a bad dream you have had and draw a picture of it. Put all the things in it that you can remember, especially the scary part. Then on another piece of paper, draw a picture of the same situation, but draw it so it's not scary anymore. After we finish the drawings, we'll talk about them.*

3. Demonstrate by drawing a picture of a nightmare that you had as a child, and then redraw it to place yourself in control.

4. As the children work, offer suggestions to those who are having difficulty, but let them work independently.

5. As they draw, praise and encourage the children for their ideas, rather than for the quality of their drawings. Ask volunteers to describe what is happening in their pictures—first the scary parts, and then how they redrew the pictures so they wouldn't have to be afraid anymore. Thank each volunteer.

Other things to try:

Have each child draw a picture of a scary nightmare and share it with the group. Then have the group brainstorm ways to change the picture to get rid of the scary parts.

Trust Walk

Activity and Debrief

What this activity teaches:

- Trust builds between people who are responsible.
- Trust can break down if someone is not responsible.

You will need:

A large room or outdoor area that offers a variety of shapes, textures, and objects for the children to explore, by touch. Blindfolds, such as scarves, dish towels, or pieces of cloth.

Directions:

1. Explain to the children that this is an activity in which partners work together to build trust. Tell them: *One partner will be blindfolded and the other will be the guide. When you are the guide, lead your "blind" partner around the room or outdoor area safely and carefully, while providing opportunities for him or her to touch different objects, listen to sounds, and smell various aromas. Don't talk during the activity. At the end of 10 minutes, I'll give a signal and you will change places with your partner. After 10 more minutes, I will signal you to return to the group to share what happened on your Trust Walk.*

2. Have the children choose partners. Tell them to decide who will be the guide and who will be the blindfolded person during the first round. Stress the responsibility of the guides to provide a lot of experiences for their partners—but in safe ways. Also remind the children that they may not talk during the exercise. Suggest that they agree on how the guide will lead the partner; for example, by holding hands or by linking arms. They may establish non-verbal signals to indicate left, right, up, down, fast, or slow.

3. Call time after the first 10 minutes so the partners can change roles, and then after the second 10 minutes, ask the children to return. **Watch the children as the do the activity to be sure that they are leading their partners in a safe manner.**

Discussion:

After each partner has had a turn to be both a blindfolded person and a guide, gather the children together for a discussion and debrief of their experiences. Ask them these questions:

— *What were some of the things you experienced on your walk?*
— *How did you feel being the guide?*
— *How did you feel being guided?*
— *What was it like to do the activity in silence?*
— *What did you learn about being responsible?*

Be Eggs-tra Careful!

Activity and Debrief

What this activity teaches:

- We can learn to be responsible for something that needs our care and protection.
- We become responsible by accepting responsibilities.

You will need:

Raw eggs (one per child), and colored magic markers.

Directions:

1. Tell the children that they are going to have the responsibility of taking care of something very fragile and delicate for one whole day. They will be given a raw egg to take with them everywhere they go for the next twenty-four hours.

2. Give each child a raw egg. Tell the children to decorate the eggs with magic markers, making sure not to break them. Have them name their eggs, and treat them like special friends. If you like, break an egg on a plate or in a bowl, to help the children see how "heartbroken" an egg becomes when it is not properly cared for.

3. Say to the children: *You must take your raw egg with you everywhere you go for the next twenty-four hours. You may set it on the table while you eat or put it on the night stand while you sleep, but you may not hide it. It is your responsibility to protect your egg from harm and keep it company. Bring it back next time we meet, to show that you kept it safe.*

Discussion:

The next time you meet, lead a discussion of the experiences the children had protecting their eggs. Ask them:

— *What did you do to protect your egg during your daily activities?*
— *What did you say to other people about your egg?*
— *Did you have any "close calls," or did you let your egg get broken?*
— *How did you feel about being in charge of something so fragile for a whole day?*
— *What did you learn about being responsible while doing this activity?*

Taking Care of Pets

Creative Role Play

What this activity teaches:

- Taking care of pets is an important responsibility.
- Assuming the care of a pet is a good rehearsal for other responsibilities in life.

You will need:

Chart paper and magic markers.

Directions:

1. In this activity, the children will assume the role of their pet, in order to understand the animal's perspective. Begin by brainstorming the kinds of pets that the children have or would like to have. List them on the board or chart paper. Then discuss the care that each animal would require in order to stay healthy and happy. Be sure to include exercise, shelter, food and water, companionship, affection, pest control, and cleanliness. This will bring to awareness the needs of each kind of animal, so that the children can more easily role play their chosen animal.

2. Ask the children to think about their own pet—or the pet they would like to have. Say to them: *Now that we have listed various kinds of pets, and the care each needs to survive and be happy, put yourself in the place of that animal and think about what it would say about you if it could talk. What would your pet turtle, Horace, say about how you care for him? Would your dog, Fluffy, say that you take her for a run every morning and evening? Do you think your guinea pig, Grover, would brag about how clean you keep his cage? Pretend you are your pet and talk with a partner who is taking the role of his or her pet.*

3. Ask volunteers to come before the group, two or three at a time, to role play their pets in an animal "chit chat." Encourage them to say what their animals would really say if they could talk. Suggest that they assume the mannerisms of the animals, but focus on how their owner or master takes care of them. Allow 1 1/2 to 2 minutes per scenario.

Discussion

After the role play, ask the children:

— *In what ways did you become more aware of the needs of your animal when you took its role?*
— *What would happen to your pet if you were not responsible in caring for it?*
— *How is having a pet a big responsibility?*

Responsible Me!

An Art Activity

What this activity teaches:

- We can become more aware of our responsibilities by picturing them.
- We are responsible in many different ways.

You will need:

Plain paper, pencils, black construction paper, white glue, colored chalk, facial tissues, and hair spray.

Directions:

1. Place the materials on a table or workspace. Tell the children that they are going to draw one of their responsibilities with glue on black paper. After the glue dries, they will fill in the spaces with colored chalk.

2. Explain: *Everyone has responsibilities. Some are big responsibilities and some are smaller responsibilities. Think of one of the ways in which you are responsible and draw it with pencil on the newsprint. For example, you might want to draw your hand holding a dog's water dish under a faucet—or yourself getting up on time in the morning. Experiment by drawing a variety of sketches. Keep your objects big and simple. When you are satisfied with a sketch, draw it on the black paper. Use the white glue to go over the pencil lines.*

3. Collect the drawings. Let the glue dry for several hours or overnight; it will be transparent when dry. Tell the children to fill in the shapes with colored chalk, using only one finger to spread the chalk evenly. They can clean their fingers with a tissue as they change chalk colors, and wash their hands when they are done. Seal the pictures with a light coating of hair spray to keep the chalk from smearing.

4. As the children work, talk about those responsibilities that they consider the most important. Ask them how they feel about what their pictures depict. Display the completed pictures around the room before sending them home with the children.

Necessary Rules
Fantasy/Group Activity

What this activity teaches:

- Most rules are necessary and helpful.
- We have reasons for the rules we establish.

You will need:

A box containing cards or slips of paper, each with a different rule written on it. (Examples are: "Trash must not be thrown out of car windows." "People may not possess illegal drugs.") Paper and pens.

Directions:

1. Introduce the activity by asking the children: *Why do we have rules or laws? Are they really necessary?*

2. Have a volunteer pull a card and read the rule on it. Ask, *What's one possible reason for this rule?* or *Why would someone have made this rule?* Lead a discussion about the importance of rules.

3. Have the children form groups of three or four. Tell them that each group is going to create an imaginary land, and establish a set of rules for the people who live there.

4. Explain: *Give your land a name, agree on what it is like, and decide who can live there. Then establish a set of rules, and decide what will happen to people who don't cooperate with those rules.*

5. As the children are creating their lands, encourage them to look at the "whys" of their rules, and at what would happen if they didn't have such rules.

6. Ask volunteers to describe their lands and the rules they established for people who live there. Take advantage of this time to discuss and reinforce specific rules that are necessary to maintaining order.

Other things to try:

In preparation for the initial discussion, instead of writing rules on cards yourself, have each of the children think of a rule and write it down.

The Rules of the Game

Game Creation and Discussion

What this activity teaches:

- In most games, rules are necessary.
- Rules help make games more fun.
- Rules sometimes need to be modified.
- We can make rules together.

You will need:

Two boxes, and various objects to place in the boxes (like whistles, balls, sticks, shoes, tools, etc.), paper, and pens.

Directions:

1. Introduce the activity by asking the children to think of some games they like to play. Pick two or three of the games they mention, and discuss the rules that govern them.

2. Divide the children into two groups, Give each group a piece of paper and pen, and a box with some objects in it.

3. Explain: *Look at the objects in your box. Your task is to create a game with those objects. Decide what rules are necessary in order for the game to work. Are there any penalties for breaking the rules? If so, what are they? Give the game a name, and write the rules on the sheet of paper. Each group will then teach the other group how to play its game, explaining the rules that govern it.*

4, During the activity, be encouraging. Offer some suggestions if the children really get stuck, but allow them as much independence as possible.

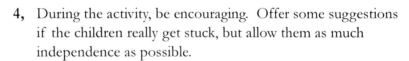

5. Have each group take a turn teaching its game and rules. Play each game for a short period of time.

Discussion:

After playing both games, talk about each of them. Ask:

— *Would any other rules help make this game more fun?*
— *Were any of the rules unnecessary?*
— *Should any of the rules be changed?*
— *Why are rules important to games?*
— *Why are rules important in life?*

What Do You Want

Art/Creative Thought

What this activity teaches:

- All of the things we want in our lives are choices we make.
- Throughout our lives, we choose what we want most— and do   what we choose.

You will need:

Enough colored notebook-size paper so that each child has three sheets. White glue, scissors, pens or pencils, and plenty of magazines that children look at or read.

Directions:

1. Place the materials on large tables and divide them evenly among the children. The children will be cutting words and pictures from the magazines and gluing them to their colored sheets of paper. They can also create drawings and designs to supplement what they find in the magazines.

2. Explain: *We are going to make pictures of the things we really, really, really want to have in our lives. Take a moment and think about what you would like most to have, to be, to see, or to do. Now, make a list of the three most important things you want. Cut out pictures and words that describe what you want from the magazines, and glue them to your paper. You have one sheet on which to show each thing you want. If you like, make drawings and designs of your own.*

3. As the children work, watch to see if you can assist anyone who is having difficulty. Let them be as creative as they wish. There is no right or wrong way to do this activity; however, the wants that the children depict need to be positive. Allow enough time for work and cleanup.

4. During the activity, assist where you can, and reassure the children that they are doing fine. Ask the children to talk about their choices, acknowledging each child with appreciation.

5. When the children have completed their three pictures, conduct a sharing session during which the children each share one of their sheets and talk about what they've chosen and why.

How to Spend Our Money
Group Choice and Presentation

What this activity teaches:

- Most choices we make involve other people, and also affect them.
- When deciding how to do things, we can usually choose from several good alternatives.

You will need:

A large bag of beans to total one hundred beans for each group of two, three, or four children. Writing paper, and pens or pencils.

Directions:

1. Have the children form groups of two, three, or four depending on the total number of children involved. At least two groups are required. Each group will receive one-hundred beans, which will become that group's treasury. Together the children will cooperate to make choices about how best to use this treasury.

2. Explain: *Each group will count out one-hundred beans from the large bag. Pretend that each bean is a dollar, so that you really have one-hundred dollars. Working individually, I want you to think of the very best way to use your group's money. Then, when we're all ready, you'll work with the others in your group to make one choice from among all of your ideas about how to use the money. When your group has made its choice, write it down.*

3. Allow two or three minutes for individual thought, and then encourage the groups to start making their group choices. Ask each group to indicate when it has completed the task. Don't proceed until all groups are finished.

4. During the activity you may want to offer some suggestions. When the groups have finished, ask each to present its choice. Be sure to acknowledge each group's efforts.

5. Have each child tell about feelings experienced in the process of reaching a group decision.

Other things to try:

Combine the small groups and see if the children can make a choice for the entire group.

Choices People Make

News Review and Discussion

What this activity teaches:

- Almost everything that happens in the world is the result of choices people make.
- Every choice we make has an outcome.
- Different choices have different outcomes.

You will need:

Current newspapers (one for every two children), scissors, writing paper, and pens or pencils.

Directions:

1. Organize the children into pairs, and give a newspaper and other materials to each pair. The children will be reviewing headlines and articles that show choices that people make, and the results or outcomes of those choices. They will cut out the articles they choose, and write down both the choice and the outcome described in each article.

2. Explain: *Work with your partner to find two articles in the newspaper. Look at the headlines. Pick one article in which a person, a group of people, or an organization made a choice that caused something good to happen. After that, find an article that describes a choice that caused something bad to happen. Cut out the articles, and write down the choice and outcome for each one.* As the children work, pass among them and give help, where needed.

Discussion:

After all pairs have finished, ask the group, What is the difference between a choice and an outcome, or result? Now ask the children to share their articles and the choices and outcomes they recorded.

After the presentations, ask the group the following questions:

— *In the articles with bad outcomes, what other choices could have been made?*
— *If another choice had been made, what might have been the outcome?*

Other things to try:

Have the children write short newspaper articles about choices they have made, and the outcomes of their choices.

Choices I Make

Log Keeping and Debrief

What this activity teaches:

- We make many choices everyday.
- Some choices are big and some are small.
- Some choices have immediate outcomes; others have outcomes for which we must wait.

Preparation:

Introduce this activity to the children in advance by saying: At our next meeting, we're going to look at the choices we make every day. To prepare for this, pick a day before our next meeting, and write a list of all the choices you make during that day.

Every time you make a choice, write it down. After each choice, write the outcome. Sometimes outcomes happen right away, like choosing something to eat and having it taste good. Sometimes outcomes don't happen for awhile. For example, when you save money to buy something, the outcome doesn't happen until enough money is saved to buy the thing you want. To help the children identify choices they may make share some choices that you often make.

See how many choices and outcomes you can write down in a day. When we meet next time, we'll talk about all the choices we made.

If possible, remind the children between meetings to complete their lists and to be sure to bring them.

Discussion:

At the next meeting, have the children share some of the choices and outcomes they recorded. After all of the children who wish to have shared, spend time discussing their experiences. Ask them:

— *Do we make some choices without thinking?*
— *What were some big choices you made?*
— *What were some little choices you made?*
— *Do you think you wrote down all of the choices you made?*
— *What were some choices you made that had immediate outcomes?*
— *What were some choices whose outcomes won't happen for awhile?*
— *Were you surprised at how many choices you made?*

I Accomplished Something
Art/ Collection Activity

What this activity teaches:

- Things we accomplish are worth remembering.
- When we accomplish things, we have a right to feel good about ourselves.

You will need:

Shoe boxes, scissors, glue, magazines, and an assortment of craft materials for decorating the shoe boxes.

Directions:

1. Place the materials where the children can work with them. Tell the children they are going to decorate shoe boxes that will contain momentos of their accomplishments.

2. Explain: *Each of you will be decorating a shoe box so that it can become a beautiful container for things that remind you of your accomplishments. You can decorate your box in any way you choose. When you're finished, tell the group why you decorated the box the way you did, and what you plan to place in the box first. You can use the box to hold pictures that remind you of special events, or ribbons and momentos of things you have won. It can hold ticket stubs or programs from events you performed in, or your report cards. It might be a report or a test on which you got a good grade. In other words, anything that reminds you of something you accomplished can be placed in the box.*

3. As the children work, suggest things they might include in their boxes. Give them a chance to remember and talk about some of their accomplishments as they decorate. Ask them how they feel about their various accomplishments.

4. Have each child share his or her completed box, and describe the first thing that will go into the box.

A Goal I Have

Brainstorm/Group Role Play

What this activity teaches:

- Excuses can prevent our reaching a goal if we let them.
- We can look for ways to succeed, rather than ways to fail.

You will need:

Paper, and pens or pencils.

Directions:

1. Gather the children together, and give them each a pen and paper. Tell them: *Today we are going to do some role-playing (acting out). We're going to look at some of the things that get in the way of our accomplishing the goals we set. On the paper, write down one goal. It could be "I want to be a straight A student," or "I want to be a famous musician (business tycoon, artist, scientist, athlete, or pilot)," or "I want to travel all over the world." Then write down some of your reasons (or excuses) for not being able to reach that goal. Some examples might be, "I don't have enough talent," or "If I can't be the best, I won't do it at all," or "I don't have enough money (or time, or energy)."*

2. As the children work, help them identify something that they would like to do or have someday. Encourage them to dream or imagine.

3. Have the children take turns reading their goals. Immediately after reading his or her goal, have each child act out all of the excuses that could stop him/her from achieving it. (You may want to demonstrate this first, and <u>really ham up your excuses</u>.) Instruct the group to be the encouragers. Get them to offer all kinds of advice on how to reach the goal. Encourage creative solutions. Don't allow negative input.

4. Keep the activity going, and encourage all of the children to get involved.

Discussion:

When the children have finished acting out their goals, ask:

— *What excuses/reasons did we use most often?*
— *Which suggestions seemed to be most helpful?*
— *What methods can we use to encourage <u>ourselves</u> to reach our goals?*

Goal-Setting Fun
Game and Discussion

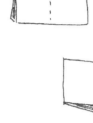

What this activity teaches:

- It helps to examine how we set and achieve goals.
- Awareness of our limits helps us set realistic goals.
- Setting realistic goals pays off.

You will need:

Many one-quarter page pieces of scrap paper, evenly cut. A stop watch, pens or pencils, and paper.

Directions:

1. Have the children sit comfortably. Give each child several sheets of paper.

2. Explain: *We're going to play a paper-folding game that will help us become better goal-setters. The object of the game is to see how many papers you can fold in a given period of time. There will be several rounds and I will give you directions for each round. Fold each paper in half, and then in half again. Keep the edges even. If more than 1/4 inch overlaps on any side, the sheet cannot be counted.* (Demonstrate, by folding a paper squarely.)

3. Start the first round, and stop it after 30 seconds. Have the children count the folded sheets according to the rules, and record the number properly folded.

4. Before round two, have each child estimate how many sheets he or she can fold in 3 minutes, based on the first round. Explain that scores which exactly match the estimate earn <u>equal points</u>. Anything over the estimate is <u>not counted</u>. And scores under the estimate earn <u>zero points</u>. Have the children write their names and estimates on paper and give them to you. Tell them to select the number of sheets that exactly matches their estimate.

5. Start the round and stop it in exactly 3 minutes. Have the children pair up and count each other's folded papers, discarding any that are not evenly folded. Have each child privately compare his or her total number of folded sheets with his or her estimate, to arrive at a score.

6. Before starting the next round, have the children form small groups and discuss the first round, by answering these questions:

   — *Did you set a goal that was:*
       a) so low you were sure to would make it?
       b) somewhat lower than you thought you could make?
       c) exactly what you thought you could make?
       d) just enough higher to provide a challenge?
       e) considerably higher than you thought you could make?
   — *What was your motive during this round?*
       a) to have fun
       b) to win
       c) to achieve the goal

7. Conduct a third round and ask these questions following the round:

   — *Did you set a more realistic goal for this round?*
   — *In what ways is your goal-setting behavior in real life similar to your goal-setting behavior in this game? In what ways is it different?*
   — *What could you do to become more effective at setting goals?*

8. Conduct a final round. This time have the children form teams of five or six. Have each team estimate how many sheets it can fold collectively—as a team—in 3 minutes. Follow the same rules and procedures as in the other rounds.

Discussion:

Afterwards, ask these questions:

   — *How did the team arrive at its goal?*
       a) majority vote
       b) consensus
       c) group average
       d) other
   — *What was the team motive during this round?*
       a) to have fun together
       b) to beat the other teams
       c) to achieve the team goal
   — *Did your group have a leader?*
   — *What things helped the group?*
   — *What things caused problems for the group?*
   — *Did you find creative or cooperative ways of working together*

Sharing Goals
Triads and Discussion:

What this activity teaches:

- Problems can arise as we work to achieve our goals.
- There are many ways to overcome obstacles to goal achievement.
- Sometimes other people come up with solutions that we don't think of ourselves.

You will need:

A space large enough to accommodate groups of three children, allowing ample space between groups.

Directions:

1. Divide the children randomly into groups of three. Have them decide who will be A, who will be B, and who will be C. (If one or two children are left over, you can assign additional C's to some groups.)

2. Explain: *Person A, you are the "goal-setter," and will state a goal that you want to achieve. Person B, you are the "discourager." You will come up with all the problems, obstacles, and roadblocks that could make achieving the goal difficult. Person C, you are the "encourager." You will offer ideas and solutions for achieving the goal. You will help remove the roadblocks. Offer any good ideas you can think of to help the goal-setter be successful. After a few minutes, I'll call time and tell you to switch roles. We will do three rounds, so that everyone can play all three roles.*

3. Choose two volunteers and demonstrate the rotation process and the goal-setter/ discourager/encourager interaction. Provide examples of goal statements, positive statements, and negative statements.

4. Lead the activity through three rounds. Circulate, and encourage the children to play their roles with enthusiasm.

Discussion:

After everyone has had a turn in each role, gather the children together and ask them:

— *What obstacles or roadblocks were mentioned most often?*
— *What were some of the best solutions offered?*
— *Do you think this activity will help you accomplish your goals? How?*

Awards for All!

Art/Awards Ceremony

What this activity teaches:

- Complimenting others and receiving recognition can be fun.
- We deserve recognition for the things we accomplish.

You will need:

Magic markers, Styrofoam cups and balls, toothpicks, wide ribbon, glue, scissors, glitter, stars, construction paper, and other supplies with which to make awards. (Some of the materials may be brought by the children.)

Directions:

1. Place the materials on a large workspace. Tell the children that they are going to create special awards for some very deserving people.

2. Explain: *Pair up with one other person, and tell him or her about an award you really want to receive. It might be the "Big Brother/Sister Award," for all the caretaking that you do, or the "Pet Owner of the Year" award, or the "Athlete of the Year" award—for making a great play in a game. It can be any award you want to receive for something that you have done in the past. Tell your partner why you deserve this award. Your partner will then make an award for you, and present it to you at the awards ceremony at the end of the meeting. When you receive your award, you may simply say "thank you," or you may give a short acceptance speech. You may not put yourself down or discount your accomplishment in any way.*

3. While the children work, offer suggestions. Help with titles for the awards, if necessary. As an example, tell the children what kind of award you would like to receive.

4. Act as the Master of Ceremonies for the event. Call each of the presenters and recipients forward for the ceremony. After each award is given, get the other children to stand and cheer. Keep it light and fun, but model serious appreciation for the children's accomplishments.

Identifying Healthy and Unhealthy Decisions

Drama and Discussion

What this activity teaches:

- We often find ourselves in situations that require us to make decisions that affect our well being.
- We can practice making healthy decisions by dramatizing real life situations with our peers.

You will need:

A copy of the real-life situations on the opposite page with each situation written on a separate page: (The number of children needed to dramatize each is shown in parentheses.)

Directions:

1. Divide the children into groups and give each group a paper with a situation written on it. Tell them that the situations are typical ones in which people must make decisions affecting their well being. Tell the children to discuss what an unhealthy, and then a healthy, decision would be in their scenario. Then have them prepare a short dramatization of each decision.

2. Have each group act out its unhealthy choice, and then its healthy one. After each drama, ask the actors how they felt acting out each situation. Talk about the consequences that each decision would have on themselves and others.

Real-Life Decision Situations:

- You come home from school with a bad headache. No one is home but you and your friend. You look in the medicine cabinet and find aspirin, Excedrin, and a prescription drug containing codeine. (2)

- A family is sitting at the dinner table and has just eaten a big turkey dinner. Everyone is full, but one person wants more, just because it tasted so good. (4-6)

- Three friends are participating in a baseball game and are awaiting their turns at bat. One friend says his feet have been itchy, and that there are cracks between his toes. One of the others has had similar symptoms for months, but has told no one. (3)

- A group of children go to a friend's house after a scout meeting. No one else is home. The friend gets into the liquor cabinet and invites the others to try some of the liquor. (4-7)

- A family is at a birthday party for a relative. It is getting late. Two of the children are sleepy, and know that they have to get up early for school the next day. The parents seem to be having a great time. (4-6)

Taking Care of Me

Discussion and Art

What this activity teaches:

- Daily personal care contributes to wellness.
- We are responsible for taking care of ourselves, in order to stay healthy.

You will need:

Chart paper, chalk, magic markers or crayons, construction paper in many colors, scissors, and glue.

Directions:

1. Invite the children to name some things that they do to contribute to their own wellness. Write them on the board or chart paper. Solicit specific examples of good hygiene, exercise, sleep, relaxation, dental care, stress management, being drug free, personal achievements, precautions with prescription drugs, nutrition, etc. Some

examples might be, "I floss my teeth daily," "I eat three nutritious meals a day," "I laugh and tell jokes to reduce stress," "I play soccer three times a week for exercise," and "I only take drugs that the doctor prescribes for me."

2. Place the materials on a table or workspace. Tell the children that they are going to create wellness emblems that symbolize the things they do to stay healthy. Each emblem will display five to eight wellness statements about each child.

3. Explain: You can make your emblem into the shape of a star with points, or a flower with petals radiating from the center. First, cut a large circle out of one color construction paper. Write your name on it in a fancy way with crayon or magic marker. Next, cut five to eight large petals or points, each out of a different color construction paper. Print a wellness statement that is true about you on each one. Choose from the ones we listed, or create new ones, but be sure that they are honest statements about how you contribute to your own health. Then glue the petals or points to the center of the circle to create a star or flower emblem. Be sure to clean up when you are finished.

4. As the children work, talk with them about how they currently take responsibility for their wellness (without reminders from parents). Ask them what they can do in the future to stay healthy.

Strategies to Manage Stress
Brainstorming and Discussion

What this activity teaches:

- The amount of control we have in stressful situations varies.
- When we have control, we can reduce stress by taking appropriate action.
- When we are not in control, we can use stress reducers.

You will need:

Chart paper and marking pens.

Directions:

1. Tell the children that the group is going to spend some time talking about stress—what it is and what can be done about it. Begin by asking the children if they ever feel uptight or on edge, get a headache or a queasy stomach. Explain that the chances are that those feelings are caused by stress. Many things can cause feelings of stress—worrying about a test, being angry at someone, being late for an important event, etc. Ask the children to think of things that cause their stress, and make a list on the chart paper.

2. After the list is complete, explain how stress works in our bodies by saying: *When we think we're in danger (of failing, being embarrassed, not getting what we want, etc.), our bodies react just like they would if we were in danger of being attacked by a lion. Adrenaline and hormones start pumping, our hearts beat faster, our muscles tense, and we get set for "fight or flight." Then if we don't take action—if we just sit around and worry, for example—all those unused hormones and tense muscles end up hurting us.*

3. Next, go through the list, one item at a time, and have the children brainstorm actions they could take in each type of situation. For example, if they are stressed because they are having problems in math, they can talk to the teacher, ask a parent for help, study with a friend, etc. Help them to understand that there are positive actions they can take to control the negative effects of stressful situations.

4. Empower the students by demonstrating enthusiasm about all the things they can do. Lead them in a rousing "I Can Do It!" Cheer after each item is discussed.

5. When the stressor is something the children have no control over (like the death of a pet) or little control over (like noisy neighbors), acknowledge that even though they can't "act on" the stressor directly, they can use stress reducers. Help the children brainstorm other stress management strategies that they can use to manage stressful feelings like listening to calming music, taking a long run, or talking to a trusted friend or adult.

6. Have the children act out some of the stressful situations and positive actions that they can take in response. Concentrate on those in which the children have some control, and encourage them to take turns dramatizing the different courses of action they could take. Lead a discussion after each dramatization that helps the children identify the value of using stress management techniques.

Imagining a Pleasant Place

Guided Imagery

What this activity teaches:

- We can create pleasant experiences in our minds.
- Taking a fantasy trip can help relieve stress.

You will need:

Watch or clock with second hand. Optional relaxing instrumental music.

Directions:

1. If you have music, start the tape at a low volume so that you can speak over it easily. Use a relaxing tone of voice. Read the following passage slowly, pausing where indicated.

2. Explain: *You are going to take a ride on an imaginary elevator. Sit or lie in a comfortable position. Be sure you are not touching anyone, and remember not to talk, whisper, or move about during the exercise. Close your eyes and relax your body. Become aware of your breathing (pause 15-20 seconds). Begin counting your breath silently in your mind (pause 45-60 seconds). Now imagine that you are standing in front of an elevator door. You press the button and the door opens, showing you a large well-lighted, empty elevator. You enter it and find that the elevator buttons are labelled as follows: The first button says, "this room;" the second button says, "a peaceful place;" the third button says, "a visit with a wise older person;" the fourth button says, "a super adventure;" and the fifth button says, "a visit with a long-lost friend." Choose the floor you would like to go to (pause 15 seconds), and press the button. The elevator door slowly closes and the elevator begins to rise to the floor you selected. The elevator arrives at the floor and the doors slowly open. Go out into the space and explore it. Meet whoever is there; do whatever makes sense for you to do there. (pause at least 60 seconds). Now say good-by to the place you're in, and to anyone who is there. The elevator has remained open for you. Enter it now. Take one last look at the place you have been. Press the button marked "this room." The elevator doors close and the elevator slowly returns you to this room (pause 15 seconds). As the elevator doors open, so do your eyes (pause until everyone's eyes are open). Welcome back!*

3. Have the children pair up. Suggest that they tell their partners as much as they would like to about their fantasies. Remind the children to listen well to each other as the fantasies are shared.

Discussion:

When the children are finished sharing, ask them:

> —*What kinds of feelings did you have during this exercise?*
> —*How can you use your imagination to reduce stress?*

Break the Stress

A Movement Game

What this activity teaches:

- Simple movements can become fun exercises.
- Movements of various kinds can be used to relieve stress.

You will need:

A large circle of chairs—one chair for each child.

Directions:

1. Ask the students to sit in a circle. Announce that the group is going to invent and practice "stress breaks" that can be used at other times to reduce stress.

2. Explain: *One of best things you can do to relieve stress is exercise. And that doesn't just mean running a mile or playing a basketball game—almost any kind of stretching or moving can help get the tension out of muscles and help you feel relaxed. Think of a movement that you can do sitting down. You can pump your arm up and down, roll your shoulders backwards and forwards; or "run" very fast with your feet. (Demonstrate several sitting movements for the children.) We're going to go around the circle and each one of you is going to lead us in a movement for 10 seconds. When it's your turn, show us a movement that no one else has done and we'll all do it with you.*

3. Get the game started and keep it going at a lively pace. Participate along with the children.

4. After every student has led a movement, tell the children to stand and move their chairs out of the way. Go around the circle again, this time creating movements that can be done from a standing position. Demonstrate a few, like running in place, stretching to the side, etc.

5. Finally, have each child lead a "traveling" movement for 5-10 seconds. Maintain the circle formation. Suggest that skipping, hopping, jogging, etc., can be done using different kinds of arm movements for variation.

Other things to try:

If you have ample space or can go outdoors, do the traveling part of the game in a snake formation, with the leader weaving about and the other children following. Include one or two short "stress breaks" at each meeting. Have the children take turns leading them.

How to Say "No!"
Skill Development

What this activity teaches:

- There are many different ways to say no.
- Most people have some degree of difficulty saying no.
- We can learn and practice refusal skills.

You will need:

Enough chairs for all of the children, placed in a circle.

Directions:

1. Have the children sit in a circle. Tell them that they are going to play a refusal skills game. Explain that the object of the game is to find out how many different ways there are to refuse, or say no when it's important to do so..

2. Explain: *When we're young, we're taught to please and obey our parents, teachers, and other adults. As a result, we learn to say yes in many different ways—but most of us don't learn how to say no very well at all. Maybe that's why saying no can be so hard for us—even as adults. We need practice at saying no to things that are harmful—and that's what this exercise is going to give us. I'm going to share with you my favorite way to say no. Then, as we go around the circle, each of you must think of a new way to say no—a way that hasn't been mentioned by anyone else. You can say no angrily, firmly, timidly, or politely. Change your facial expressions; use different words, stand up, stomp your foot, or whatever. We'll keep going around the circle for as long as we can think of new ways to say no.*

3. Offer more examples if you think the children need them. Then start the game. Encourage the children to dramatize their methods of saying no. Every time it's your turn, model the use of non-verbal behaviors along with your verbal ways of saying no. Don't stop until the group has run out of ideas.

Discussion:

Lead a discussion about the importance of developing refusal skills. Ask these questions and others:

— *What is meant by the term "refusal skill?"*
— *Why is it important to spend time practicing refusal skills?*
— *Why is it hard to say no to an adult? To a friend?*

Say "No"...And Mean It! – Part I

Role Playing and Skill Development

What this activity teaches:

- One way to resist a determined person is with equal or greater determination.
- Saying no is a skill that can be learned.

You will need:

Chart paper and magic marker. A watch or clock with a second hand.

Directions:

1. Remind the children of the previous activity in which they shared as many ways as they could think of to say no . Tell them that in this follow-up activity, they'll practice resisting a person who <u>won't take no for an answer.</u>

2. Explain: *One reason saying no doesn't always work, is that the person we're saying no to often doesn't accept our refusal. Instead, he or she keeps trying to convince us to do the thing we don't want to do. You've probably been in this sort of situation many times—trying to resist a brother, sister, or friend who pleads, and argues, and tries to get you to change your mind.* Act out a familiar example, such as one child persistently urging another to come over to his or her house.

3. Ask the children to pair up and sit facing each other. Have them decide who will be the Convincer and who will be the Resister in the first round. List several starter situations on chart paper or the board, such as:
   — Go to the movie I want to see.   — Let me copy your home work.
   — Bully a new kid.   — Take out the trash for me.
   — Steal a candy bar.   — Smoke this cigarette.

4. Coach the Convincers to try anything they can think of to get a yes answer. Tell the Resisters to keep resisting, no matter what. The livelier this exercise gets, the better. Encourage enthusiastic role playing. Allow at least 1 minute for each round. Then have the children switch roles and pick a new topic from the list.

Discussion:

At the conclusion of the exercise, ask the group these and other questions:

- *How did you feel as the Convincer?*
- *How did you feel when you were saying no?*
- *Did you feel like you had to explain your reasons for saying no?*
- *Did resisting get any easier as you continued to do it?*
- *Why is it important to practice saying "No"?*

Say "NO!"...And Mean It – Part II

Role Play and Skill Development

What this activity teaches:

- There are many ways to resist peer pressure.
- Practicing different methods of resistance can help us prepare for real life situations.

You will need:

Copies of the scenarios on the following page on individual sheets of paper.

Directions:

1. Tell the children that they're going to get another chance to test their resistance skills—this time against more than one Convincer. Get volunteers to act out one scenario at a time. Choose an additional volunteer to direct each scenario, coaching the actors to play their roles with conviction.

2. Allow different children to take the lead role (the Resister) in each scenario. Analyze and compare the resistance/refusal skills demonstrated by each.

Discussion:

After all of the scenarios have been dramatized, and every child has had a chance to be the Resister at least once, talk about the experience. Ask these and other questions:

— *How did it feel to resist several people at once?*
— *What techniques seemed to work best?*
— *Why is it hard to say no to friends?*
— *What can you do to get better at saying "No"?*

Say "NO!"…And Mean It – Role-Play Scenarios

- Bobby plays in a local baseball league. During Tuesday's practice, he injures his shoulder. At home that night, he tells his older brother, Dennis, that he's afraid he won't be able to play in Saturday's big game. Two friends of Dennis, who are there at the time, offer Bobby some steroids. They insist that the steroids will heal his shoulder fast. Dennis agrees.

- Chris, Donna, and Susan are sitting around in Jan's bedroom, talking. Susan gets out a pack of cigarettes and offers one to each girl. Susan and Jan light up. Chris and Donna have never smoked, and the other girls try to convince them to try it. Chris is tempted, and says she'll do it if Donna will. Donna is starting to feel sick from the smoke.

- Eric is walking home from school. He stops at the corner store for a soda and runs into Carlos, Jeff, Maria, and Michele. They talk and joke for awhile outside the store, and then start walking together. Jeff leads the group into an alley and lights up a marijuana cigarette. Maria and Carlos each take a drag. Michele doesn't seem to like what's happening but doesn't say anything. Eric knows it's wrong but wants to be part of the group. Carlos offers him a drag.

Speak Clearly!

Skits and Discussion

What this activity teaches:

- Many difficulties between people result from faulty communication.
- Faulty communication usually results from 1) lack of communication, or 2) unclear communication.
- To communicate well, we need to say what we mean, and mean what we say.

You will need:

Copies of the experience sheet entitled, *How Can You Say It Clearly?* (one per child).

Directions:

1. Begin by talking with the children in a general way about how much people depend on their ability to communicate with each other. Mention how communication is one of those things that can be very good or very bad. Bad communication causes misunderstandings and other problems. Bad communication can result from unclear communication, or no communication at all.

2. Distribute the experience sheets. Ask the children to read the descriptions of the two situations with you. Tell the children that you'd like them to fill in the speech bubbles of the cartoon characters after they role play the situations. Ask the children to read the descriptions of the two situations with you.

3. Have the children form small groups of three to five. Tell them that they are going to act out the situations in the cartoons. Have half of the groups act out the first cartoon. Assign the second cartoon to the other half.

4. Explain: *I'd like each group to plan and rehearse two short skits. In the first skit, act out the situation the way it is written, showing how poor communication caused problems. In the second skit, have the characters communicate better, so that no problems occur.* **5.** Give the children about 10 - 15 minutes to plan and rehearse their skits and to decide how their characters are going to demonstrate good communication. Then ask them to perform for the total group.

Discussion:

At the end of each small group's second skit, ask the children:

- *What was the cause of the problem in the first skit?*
- *Can you think of other things that could be done in the second skit to improve communication?*
- *Do any of these situations remind you of times when you were involved in a misunderstanding? What happened?*
- *Why do you think it's important to communicate clearly?*

How Can You Say It Clearly?

Experience Sheet

Here are two situations in which kids are not communicating well. Read each one. Then follow the directions—and help them communicate better!

Situation 1: Randy and Sue like each other, but both are a little shy. Sue just got a new haircut, and Randy thinks it's cute. When she looks at him, he says, "Hey, your hair is short and it's too neat!" He sticks his fingers in her hair and messes it up. The other kids laugh. Sue moves away quickly. She thinks to herself, "I guess Randy doesn't like my new haircut, and he doesn't seem to like me anymore either."

What could Randy say instead? What would Sue say to him? Fill in the bubbles.

Situation 2: Bill and Bud are pals. They decide to go on a five mile hike to the top of a big hill. They agree to meet at the one mile point. Bill says, "It's going to be great! I'll bring some stuff." Bud says, "Yeah, that's good. So will I." They meet at the right place at the right time, but each boy has a blanket and a snake bite kit. Neither has food or water, and they are already hungry and thirsty.

What <u>could</u> Bill and Bud say to each other to make a better plan? Fill in the bubbles.

Giving Precise Directions

Practice and Discussion

What this activity teaches:

- We can communicate very clearly and precisely.
- We can prevent many problems and difficulties by using communication that is clear and precise.

You will need:

An outdoor or indoor area with numerous large objects, such as plants, furniture and/or trash cans.

Directions:

1. Set up an obstacle course using the plants, furniture, trash cans, etc. This will be the "runway" over which the "pilots" in this activity must be guided.

2. Talk with the children about how important it is for people to communicate clearly and accurately. Ask them to imagine what would happen if airplane pilots didn't communicate clearly with air traffic controllers, or quarterbacks didn't communicate accurately with their football teams. Airplanes would crash, and football teams wouldn't be able to run their plays.

3. Blindfold one child and spin him or her around at one end of the runway. This person is the pilot. Station a second child at the other side of the runway—the pilot's destination. Announce that this person is the air traffic controller.

4. Explain: *When you are the air traffic controller, it is your job to guide the pilot step-by-step through the obstacles using words only. If the pilot touches anything, it counts as a crash, and your turn is over. The pilot may direct questions to the air traffic controller. The rest of us will be very quiet during the exercise.*

5. Give everyone a chance to try both roles. If you have a large group, you can set up more than one "runway" and have two or more groups doing the activity at the same time.

Discussion:

After everyone has had a turn, ask the children:

- *What can we learn from this experiment?*
- *What are some examples of other situations in which it would be essential to communicate very clearly?*
- *How can we communicate clear and exact messages?*
- *Have you ever had an experience where communicating clearly was very important? …Explain.*

Other things to try:

Ask a pilot, air traffic controller, or quarterback to visit the group. Encourage the children to ask questions about how the guest communicates precisely with others on the job. Urge the visitor to give a few examples of precise communication.

Encouraging Words

Art Activity

What this activity teaches:

- The messages we give ourselves can determine whether we succeed or fail.
- It's OK to say positive things about ourselves.

You will need:

Poster paper and magic markers in various colors.

Directions:

1. Explain to the children that positive self-talk consists of encouraging words that we say to ourselves that help us succeed. Encouraging words are helpful and powerful, particularly when we put them into positive statements about ourselves. They are especially helpful when we are feeling discouraged, or have some negative feelings about being able to accomplish something.

2. Explain: *Think of three strong, positive statements about yourself, such as "I am a good athlete," "I work hard," or "I am a great listener." Your statements should be about things that you want to become skillful at—rather than things you are already skillful at.*

3. Pass out the materials, and have the children write their statements in large letters on the poster paper. Tell them to use the magic markers to make their statements colorful and decorative. Prepare a statement yourself to show as an example. Tell the children to take their statements home and place them on a wall, or in another location where they will see them often. Tell them that each time they look at their statements, they will become more and more like them.

4. While they work, talk to the children about encouraging words, and how they can help us become more positive and capable. Assist any children who get stuck, or inadvertently include something negative in their statements. Reinforce the children for the positive statements they make. Point out that although sometimes we're told it's impolite or conceited to say good things about ourselves, these encouraging statements are not like that. They are to help the us do things we want to do.

5. When the children have completed their statements, have them each choose one statement and then share what they have written with the rest of the group. Thank each child for sharing and encourage each child to remember and believe in their encouraging words.

Listening Like a Tape Recorder

Dyads and Discussion

What this activity teaches:

- Listening well is an important skill.
- We all like to be listened to when we speak.
- People know you have listened to them if you repeat some of the things you heard them say.

Directions:

1. Talk with the children about how communication involves two functions: 1) giving, and 2) receiving messages. We give messages by speaking, and we receive them by listening. In order to be effective communicators, we have to perform both functions well.

2. Explain: *Let's see how good we are at receiving messages. I have an activity in mind that will give us a chance to see how well we can listen. The activity is called, "Listening Like a Tape Recorder." You will try to "tape record" in your mind what someone says, and then tell that person what you heard, to see if you got it right.*

3. Ask the children to form teams of two and sit in chairs with team members facing each other. Have them decide who is A and who is B. Tell the children that they are going to take turns listening to each other. Each team member will have a chance to speak and to listen. Explain: *When you are the listener you'll act like a tape recorder and try to remember everything the speaker said, but you won't ask any question. Just listen.* Direct the children through this process:

    First minute: A speaks. (Assign a topic from the list on the opposite page)

    Second minute: B "plays back" what she or he heard A say just like a tape recorder.

    Third minute: A compliments B for listening and makes any needed corrections.

    Fourth minute: B speaks. Same topic, or a new one you choose.

    Fifth minute: A "plays back" what she or he heard B say just like a tape recorder.

    Sixth minute: B compliments A for listening and makes any needed corrections.

4. If the children would like to repeat the activity, ask them to change partners. Then guide them through the same process, choosing other topics from the list.

Discussion:

Ask the children:

— *How did you feel when you listened like a tape recorder?*
— *How did you feel when you were the speaker, and were listened to so well?*
— *How did you know you were listened to?*
— *Why is listening without interrupting the speaker an important part of good communication?*

Other things to try:

Suggest that the children try listening very carefully to other people, letting them know they are being heard by repeating back to them some of the things they say. Suggest that they use lead-ins like this: *I believe I really heard you, Mom. You said that...*

Tape recorder topics:

- Something that makes me happy
- A special person in my life
- My favorite song
- My favorite TV show
- Something I want to do someday
- Something I do to keep a friend
- A way I show respect for others
- What I like about my favorite game

Dear Me . . .
Letter-Writing Activity

What this activity teaches:

- It is important to be positive with ourselves.
- We can encourage ourselves in fun ways.
- We are subject to many negative influences, and we can take steps to counteract them.

You will need:

A Copy of the experience sheet, *What to Say to Yourself*, for each child. Writing paper and pens or pencils. One envelope for each child.

Directions:

1. Pass out the experience sheets, writing paper, and pencils to the children. Review the directions, and have the children complete their experience sheets. As they are working, walk around and assist the children as necessary.

2. When the children have completed the experience sheets, tell the children that they are now going to write a very special letter to themselves. They are to be exceedingly complimentary, and include all the encouraging words they can think of. The letter should contain only positive comments and remarks—nothing negative or discouraging. It should recognize their good traits, attributes, and accomplishments, and should inspire them to keep working on areas in which they want to improve. Set the tone by sharing several sample sentences with the children.

3. Pass out additional paper and pencils along with the envelopes. Tell the children to begin writing. While the children are busy writing, circulate and offer assistance. Remind them of how important their words are, and how they are affected by them. Point out that since the media (television, newspapers, the internet, etc.) and people at times seem to bombard us with negatives, we need all the positive input we can get.

4. When they are finished, have them address their envelopes. Collect the letters, and put them away in a safe place for three months. At the end of three months, pass out the envelopes to the children and have them read what they wrote and talk about the importance of talking positively to ourselves.

What to Say to Yourself

Experience Sheet

Sometimes other people say discouraging words to us. And sometimes, we say discouraging words to ourselves, too. When we listen to discouraging words, we begin to have doubts about ourselves. That's when we need help.

Try this:

On a separate piece of paper, write down 3 of the most negative things you've ever said to yourself—or that someone else has said to you.

Now rewrite those negative statements, so that they are positive and encouraging.
Example: *I'm just no good at math.*
Change to: *Math problems are easy and fun to solve.*

1._____

_____

2._____

_____

3._____

_____

Now do this:

Take the paper with the discouraging words on it, and shred it into bits. As you throw the bits of paper away, tell yourself that you are throwing away all those discouraging thought and beliefs. They are gone.

And this:

Think about the positive statements you wrote here, and refer back to these statements when you need encouragement.

Go Fly a Kite

Craft Activity

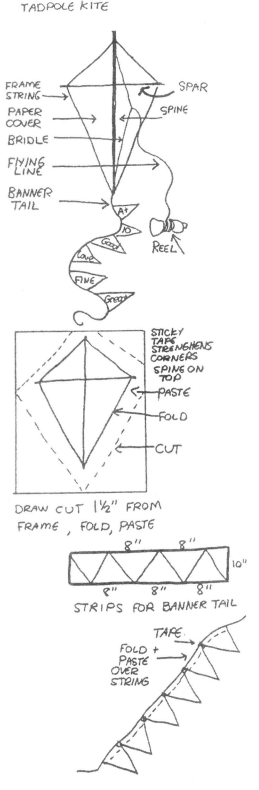

TADPOLE KITE

FRAME STRING
PAPER COVER
BRIDLE
FLYING LINE
BANNER TAIL

SPAR
SPINE
REEL

STICKY TAPE STRENGHENS CORNERS SPINE ON TOP
PASTE
FOLD
CUT

DRAW CUT 1½" FROM FRAME, FOLD, PASTE

8"   8"
10"
8"   8"   8"
STRIPS FOR BANNER TAIL

TAPE.
FOLD + PASTE OVER STRING

What this activity teaches:

- We can encourage ourselves and others in many different situations.
- We can affect our own attitudes by our words or thoughts.
- By following directions and experimenting appropriately, we can complete a complicated task .

You will need:

Scissors, ruler, pencil, paste, 3/4-inch transparent mending tape, glue, marking pens, and a sharp pocket knife (to be used by the adults only!). For each kite: light-weight white or brown wrapping paper; 300 feet of strong, soft white cotton household string; an empty plastic bottle or wide piece of wood for line reel; one 21-inch piece of split bamboo stake notched at each end for the spar; and another 28-inch piece also notched at each end for the spine.

Directions:

1. Gather the children together and tell them that they are going to build tadpole kites. Have them choose partners. Try to pair older children with younger children. Urge the children to follow the directions precisely, and to be careful with the tools and materials. Make your kite beforehand, so you will be prepared to demonstrate each step of the kite building process.

2. Give each child one 21-inch and one 28-inch stick, and tell them: *Find and mark the center of the short stick (spar). Measure and mark 7 inches from one end of the long stick (spine). Make a cross with the short stick centered 7 inches from the top of the long stick. Bind the intersection with string and then glue it. Then use a 10-foot long piece of string to frame the kite. Start with the notched end of one stick, and in sequence, attach the string to the remaining notched ends of both sticks. Be sure to keep the framing string taut, and maintain the cross (the intersection of the sticks) at right angles.*

3. *Cut wrapping paper to cover the frame. Use the framed cross as a pattern. Allow the paper to extend 1-1/2 inches beyond the frame on all sides. Fold the extensions over the frame string and paste. Cut a 40-inch string for the bridle (this holds the kite at the correct angle to the wind). Tie the ends of the bridle to the top and bottom of the spine. Leave about 8 inches of slack in the bridle.*

4. *The paper tail (which keeps the tadpole kite upright) will need to be 4 to 7 times the length of the spine, depending on the wind strength. To make a banner tail, cut 35 triangular flags from 10-inch wide strips of wrapping paper (see diagram on previous page). Using marking pens, write encouraging words or positive statements on each of the flags. Paste them to the tail string by folding the wide ends over the string. Place a piece of tape between each flag to prevent tearing.*

5. *Attach the free end of the remaining string (for flying the kite) to the bridle. The initial attachment should be 8 inches from the top end of the bridle string. Place mending tape on either side of the attachment will keep the string from slipping.*

6. Go fly the kites. Select an area where the kites will be clear of power lines, trees, and people. Open parks, beaches, or playgrounds are good places to fly. Carry a repair kit: Take a pocket knife, scissors, roll of mending tape, paper for patching, and extra string. With a tadpole kite, it is important to have plenty of extra tail material in case the tail must be extended.

7. To launch the kite: Have the children stand with their backs to the wind, and hold their kites up to catch the wind. As the wind takes the kites up, tell the children to let out more line. To avoid painful cuts, caution the children not to let the line run too quickly through their fingers.

8. Adjusting the rigging: The stronger the wind, the longer the tail must be to keep it steady. Show the children how to move the towing position up or down the bridle string to change the kite's angle of attack to the wind. The stronger the wind, the higher the towing position.

Discussion:

After the kite fly, lead the children in a discussion concerning their efforts. Ask them:

— *What did you enjoy most about this activity?*
— *Do you think that you could build another kite? How would you make the second kite better than the first one?*
— *What encouraging words did you say to yourself as you attempted to get your kite airborne?*
— *If your kite didn't fly or didn't fly very long, what kinds of things did you say to yourself?*
— *What encouraging words did you say to others?*

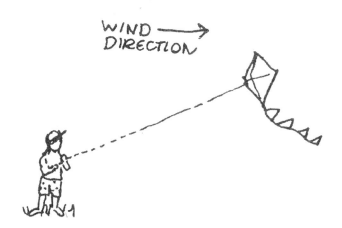

Acting Out Emotions
Role Play and Observation

What this activity teaches:

- We can sometimes determine emotions with only minimum clues.
- Most emotions can be conveyed in several ways.
- We can be careful observers.

You will need:

Three boxes or other containers. In the first box, place approximately 15 slips of paper on which you have written the names of emotions or moods, such as mad, sad, furious, irate, happy, etc. (It's OK to repeat emotions, but include as many different ones as you can.) In the second box, place approximately 10 slips of paper on which you have written body parts, such as arms, shoulders, feet, and head (these too can be repeated). In the third box, place about 5 slips of paper on which you have written different roles, such as teacher, parent, coach, bus driver, counselor, grandmother, or friend.

Directions:

1. Gather the children together and tell them: *Today you are going to have a chance to do some role playing, but you are not going to use any words. You will use only your body to get the message across. And when it's your turn to take part in a role play, you'll do it with your back to the rest of us. We will try to guess what emotion you are acting out.*

2. Choose three volunteers for the first role play. Have them silently draw one slip from the emotion box, turn their backs to the group, and independently (and nonverbally) act out the emotion they've drawn. The three volunteers will be acting out the same emotions. Ask the group to guess what emotion is being dramatized. Ask for new volunteers and do two or three more rounds like this one.

3. Next, have the players draw both an emotion and a body part. This time when they turn their backs to the group, they must act out the emotion using only that one body part. Do three or four rounds in this manner, with the large group guessing the emotion.

4. Finally, have the players draw both an emotion and a role; for example, "mad" and "grandmother." Repeat the procedure described above.

Discussion:

Following the activity, generate a discussion by asking these and other questions:

— *Were you surprised that you could correctly identify emotions from the back? . . .from the movement of only one body part?*

— *Which emotions or moods were the toughest to determine?*

— *What were some of the main indicators of anger? fear? sadness? etc.*

How Feelings Look
Movement/Observation Activity

What this activity teaches:

- We can learn to recognize people's feelings from their nonverbal behaviors.
- Individuals react nonverbally in similar ways when each is presented with the same situation.

You will need:

The list of situations from the opposite page, each of which generates a different emotion or reaction.

Directions:

1. Ask the children to form a circle. Have them extend their arms outward and touch each other's outstretched hands. This will allow plenty of space for movement.

2. Explain: *When I call out a situation, you must respond nonverbally in a way that seems appropriate to that situation. For example, if I say, "You have just won the lottery," you might do this: (Demonstrate by jumping up and down, waving your arms, or letting your mouth drop open). Now show me how you would respond to the lottery example. While you are reacting, notice the reactions of others too.*

3. Encourage the children to really "get into it."

4. Call out another situation from the list. Allow enough time for the children to respond. Remind them to respond nonverbally, and to look around and make mental note of the different ways in which the other children respond.

5. Continue calling out situations until you have exhausted the list.

Discussion:

Generate a discussion by asking these and other questions:

> — *What kinds of actions or gestures were used for positive reactions? For negative reactions?*
> — *Can you recall seeing someone react differently than you did to the same situation?*
> — *What did you notice about people's facial expressions?*

Other things to try:

Have the children call out their own situations, or simply feelings that can be expressed nonverbally.

Situations for How Feelings Look

- Your mom just said you can have a puppy.

- Your teacher just caught you looking on someone else's test paper.

- The ball you threw in a game just broke a window.

- You just broke your moms favorite dish.

- You're home alone and you hear strange noises outside your bedroom window.

- Your soccer team just won the tournament.

- You just stubbed your toe.

- Your best friend just moved to another city.

- You have just been given a good citizenship award by your principal.

- You're in a bike race and you just got a flat tire.

- You just found out that you got an "A+" on a very important test.

Walk a Mile in My Moccasins

Experiment, Dyads, and Discussion

What this activity teaches:

- Understanding each other's experiences takes effort.
- We all deserve understanding and respect.

You will need:

An extra pair of socks for each child (optional).

Directions:

1. Have the children form a circle. Explain that they are going to find out what it feels like to walk in someone else's shoes. Tell them to count off by two's. Ask the 2's to remove one shoe and place it in the center of the circle. Tell all of the children to close their eyes. While their eyes are closed, mix up the shoes. Then tell the 1's to reach in and take the first shoe they touch. Tell the children to open their eyes.

2. Explain: *Find the person whose shoe you have. Put on both of your partner's shoes, while he or she puts on your shoes. If you're not wearing socks, use one of the extra pairs I've provided. If you are wearing socks, but would like to wear an extra pair over your own, that's OK too. Now, take a short walk with your partner and talk about what it's like to wear each other's shoes. If the shoes are too small for you, notice what that feels like, and do the best you can.*

3. Allow the children to walk and talk for five to ten minutes. Then, still wearing each other's shoes, have the partners sit together and take turns sharing in response to one of the following topics:
   - *A Time I Was Misunderstood*
   - *I Was Treated Unfairly Because I'm Different*

4. Tell the children that when it is their turn to listen, they are to be very attentive and do their best to understand their partner's experience. When their partner is finished speaking, they are to say very firmly and warmly, "I understand." Allow about two minutes of sharing per child.

Discussion:

Have the children form a large group and ask:

— *How did you feel when you were wearing your partner's shoes?*
— *Did you learn anything new about your partner?*
— *Why is it important to try to understand each other's experiences and differences?*

A Mixed Bouquet of People

Art Activity

What this activity teaches:

- There are many unique varieties of flowers and people.
- Combining different kinds of flowers and people can produce interesting and beautiful results.

You will need:

Colored poster paper, magazines containing photos and illustrations of people and flowers (National Geographic would be excellent), scissors, glue, and magic markers in various colors. A bouquet containing several different kinds of flowers (optional).

Directions:

1. Begin this activity by talking to the children about the enormous varieties of flowers that are available to grow, or to buy from the florist. Point out that if they were to go to a florist, they could choose a bouquet made up of only one type of flower, or they could choose a mixed bouquet. Talk about the advantages of choosing a mixed bouquet. Mention that the variety of colors, shapes, textures, and scents would be beautiful, interesting, and stimulating to the senses. (If you brought a bouquet of flowers, use it as an example.)

2. Compare variety in flowers to variety in people. Point out that the different personalities, colors, backgrounds, religions, and talents in people are even more exciting.

3. Divide the children into groups of three or four, and distribute the materials. Tell the children that each group is going to make two mixed bouquets—one of flowers, and one of people.

4. Explain: *Look through the magazines, and cut out pictures of different kinds of people, and different kinds of flowers. Find as much variety as you can. On one sheet of poster paper, arrange a collage of the people in the shape of a bouquet. On the other sheet of poster paper, do the same with the flowers. When you have finished your arrangements, glue the pictures down. Use the magic markers to draw a vase, and to attach a stem with leaves to each person or flower. Complete the collages by adding additional decorations with the magic markers.*

5. Circulate and talk with the children while they are creating. Ask them to guess where the people in their pictures work and live, and how they think the people would get along if they knew they were all part of the same bouquet. Talk about the richness that results from combining many unique individuals—whether they are people or flowers.

6. When the collages are done, put them up for all to see.

We're the Same and Different

Activity and Discussion

What this activity teaches:

- We are all different, but we are also the same.
- Sometimes people don't accept each other's differences.
- We can be more tolerant and accepting of each other's differences if we try to understand each other.

You will need:

Chart paper and magic marker.

Directions:

1. Have the children sit in a circle and discuss the many ways in which people are different.

2. On the chart paper, write these terms: *race, religion, gender, handicap, ethnicity, economic level, place of residence, education, values.*

3. Discuss the meaning of the terms, giving several examples of each. Point out that these are some of the major ways in which people are different.

4. Have the children pair up with the person next to them. Tell them to turn toward each other, without leaving the large circle. Say: *Look at your partner. Notice as many things as you can about your partner that are different from you. Tell your partner one of the things you notice. Listen while she or he tells you how you are different.*

5. Now, ask the children to think about the ways in which they and their partners are the same, and take turns describing to the partner one of those similarities.

Discussion:

After you have finished, ask the children:

— *How do people react to these differences in others?*
— *What would the world be like if we were all the same?*
— *How do you feel when you are with someone who is different from you?*
— *If you feel uncomfortable around someone who is different from you, what can you do about it?*
— *How do you feel when someone puts you down because you are different?*

Living with a Disability
Experiment and Discussion

What this activity teaches:

- Living with a disability requires making many adjustments in daily activities.
- Experiencing a disability can help us appreciate abilities and conveniences we normally take for granted.
- People with disabilities are just like us, and deserve respect and consideration, just like we do.

You will need:

Ear plugs, crutches, bandages or cloths to use as slings; surgical tape, pieces of lightweight wood or plastic to use as splints; and one or more wheelchairs, if you can obtain them. Adult volunteers to accompany the children on the field trip portion of the activity.

Directions:

1. Tell the children that they are going to get a very small taste of what it's like to have a disability. They can be deaf, speech impaired (with mouth partially or completely taped), or "lose" an arm, leg, or both legs. Explain that while they have a disability they will continue with their regular group activities. They will have a chance to experience what sorts of adjustments they have to make in their normal behavior in order to participate in routine activities.

2. Have each child choose a partner, and pick a handicap. If one member of a pair decides to experience a hearing loss by wearing ear plugs, the other should choose something different, like the "loss" of an arm. This way the children can compensate for each other's limitations, which will ensure that the experiment is a safe one.

3. Have the children splint, bandage, and otherwise prepare each other for the experiment.

4. When everyone is ready, conduct a regular session, doing all the things you would normally do. Tell the children to be alert to all aspects of the experience, so that they will be prepared to talk about it at the end of the day.

Discussion:

At the end of your day, use these and other questions to spark a discussion:

— *What kinds of things did you have to do to adjust to your disability?*
— *How did other people treat you?*
— *What was it like going through doors? . . . going to the bathroom? . . . passing other people?*
— *What effect did this experience have on your attitudes toward people with disabilities?*

The Support of Friends

A Cooperative Game

What this activity teaches:

- Friends who cooperate and support each other make life easier and more enjoyable for each other.
- Supporting each other can be fun, and it can be difficult.

You will need:

An outdoor space, free of glass, rocks, or holes; or an indoor space with mats or carpeting.

Directions:

1. Brainstorm with the children ways in which friends give each other support. Include suggestions such as, "encouraging friends to do their best in a ball game or race," "helping friends with chores or homework," and "sharing P.E. equipment." Also include "listening to friends when they have important things to say," "sharing feelings," and "consoling friends when they are upset." Discuss with the children how they feel when supported by their friends in these ways.

2. Tell the children that they are going to play a game in which they give each other physical support. It is a fun game in which friends may end up struggling, stumbling, and giggling, as well as supporting each other. They will start with one partner, and add another each time they accomplish their task. Say to them: *You will begin the game by sitting on the ground, back-to-back with your partner, knees bent and elbows linked. All you have to do is stand up together. With a little practice and cooperation, it will be pretty easy.*

3. After the partners have mastered standing up back-to-back, have some of them divide and join other partners to make groups of three, with the same task. Then try groups of four, five, and so on. A whole group stand-up can be achieved by having everyone sit close and stand up quickly, at exactly the same moment.

4. Expect a lot of giggling and falling over. Don't be concerned if the large group stand-up doesn't work. The fun is in the trying.

Discussion:

After groups of various numbers have made several attempts to stand up, gather the children together and talk about how they felt when they were able to stand up together. Ask them:

— *How did it feel to support each other, and cooperate with one another?*
— *Was it easy to do every time? …Explain.*
— *How is this physical game of support like being supportive of friends in other ways?*

88

Helping, Not Hurting a Friend

Role Play and Discussion

What this activity teaches:

- We can all get hurt when a friend treats us badly.
- We can lose friends by treating them badly.
- We can keep friends by treating them kindly.

You will need:

Pieces of paper with the following situations written on them:

1. Tattling on a friend or friends
2. Saying something hurtful to a friend
3. Gossiping about a friend or friends to other people
4. Embarrassing your friend or friends in front of other people
5. Laughing at a friend because he or she has new glasses, a new haircut, braces, etc.

Directions:

1. Tell the children that they will be asked to divide into small groups and act out imaginary situations that they would avoid engaging in if they wanted to keep a friend.

2. Ask the children to divide into groups of three or four. Have each group draw one sheet of paper with a situation written on it. Tell the groups that they will have 5 - 10 minutes to create and rehearse a short skit based on their scenarios. Observe the rehearsals, and make sure that the children playing the part of the friend in each scenario react to what is said or done that is mean and hurtful.

3. When the children have finished rehearsing, have each group take a turn acting out its scenario. Show your appreciation; clap after each scene is over.

Discussion:

After each role play, ask the children:

— *What did the person or persons in this scenario do to hurt a friend or friends?*
— *Would you behave like this if you wanted to keep a friend?*
— *How would you feel if a friend treated you like this?*
— *How would you change this situation so that the person could keep his or her friends?*

Creating a String Painting

Art Activity

What this activity teaches:

- We can learn to work together by doing something fun.
- Accomplishing a task with a partner requires cooperation.

You will need:

White construction paper, one 2-foot piece of string per child, and tempera paint in several colors.

Dip string in paint Jar.

making design

Fold paper over and press down - pull string out.

Directions:

1. Tell the children that each of them, along with a partner, is going to participate in a cooperative art activity. Partners can make two paintings so that each child can take home one of them. Before the activity begins, have the children pair up. If there is an extra person, you can be his or her partner.

2. Place the materials on large workspaces. Have each pair decide on two colors for its string painting. Contrasting colors, such as red and blue, or a light and dark color, work best. Tell the children: *First, fold your drawing paper in half. Then reopen it. One of you will dip your string into a color of paint, holding onto one end of the string. Carefully place the painted string on one half of the paper, creating some kind of a design. Keep holding the dry end of the string, and let it stick out of the paper, while your partner folds the other half of the paper over the string. Your partner will then press lightly with his or her hands on the outside of the paper while you pull out the string. Open the paper. Next, your partner will repeat the process with his or her string, using another color of paint, and will make a design over yours while you press on the paper.*

3. The result will be a beautiful two-color butterfly, with one color underneath the other. Let each team make two paintings. Be sure to allow time for clean up.

4. As the children work, ask them how they feel about creating a piece of art as a team. *Do they need to have some special talent to do this? Do they need to cooperate to accomplish the task? Is it fun?* Have the partners share their paintings with the group.

Other things to try:

See if the partners would like to "dance" their paintings. Have them notice how the two colors relate to each other on the paper. What shapes and directions do they take? Play some music and let the partners choreograph their string paintings.

The Human Helping Machine
Creative Movement and Problem Solving

What this activity teaches:

- We can work cooperatively to solve problems.
- When one person in a group experiences difficulties, everyone has a responsibility to offer help and support.

Directions:

1. Divide the children into groups of four or five. Announce that each group will design a Human Helping Machine to "solve" a particular world problem.

2. Prepare a list of world problems in advance and post them, or allow the groups to brainstorm their own problems. Examples are: abolishing war, eliminating world hunger, eradicating crime, and curing disease. It's OK if more than one group chooses the same problem.

3. Explain: Each member of your group will be a machine part, and all of the parts must work together. Each part must move, make a noise, and have a function in the problem-solving. For example, you might be a part that bobs up and down, making a slurping noise as it gobbles up all the nuclear warheads in the world. You must move around, but you cannot get more than an arm's length away from the other parts (people) that make up your machine. Before you start building, get together and decide what problem you want to solve, and how each of you will function within the machine that solves it.

4. As soon as the machines are all "up and running," have each group demonstrate its machine to the total group. While the machine is working, walk up and touch one member of the group. Tell the children that the part you touched is now malfunctioning. Direct the other members of the group to try to help that part, while continuing their own functioning. Allow them to assist the malfunctioning part for at least 1 minute. If time allows, cause another part of the machine to malfunction.

5. **Optional:** Have the groups merge and work cooperatively to solve a single problem. Members must still have unique noises, movements, and functions.

Practice Giving An "I" Message

Drama and Discussion

What this activity teaches:

- Taking responsibility for one's own actions, feelings, and opinions can be one of the best ways to ease tense situations.
- Starting sentences with the word "I" instead of the word "you" can show one's willingness to take responsibility.

You will need:

The Experience Sheets entitled, *Don't Say "You," Say "I"* (one per child).

Directions:

1. Begin by telling the children about two different ways that a person can respond to tense situations. A person can say, "You . . .," or a person can say "I . . ." When you start a sentence with the word, you, it's a "you" message. When you start a sentence with the word I, it's an "I" message. "You" messages often lead to blaming and name calling. For example: You did it, you dope! "I" messages are usually more tactful. For example: I didn't mean to hurt you. I regret what happened.

2. Distribute the Experience Sheets to the children. Tell them to fill in the speech bubbles on their own after you do the activity together. Ask them to read the descriptions of the two situations with you. Choose four volunteers to play the parts of the individuals in the two cartoons (two per cartoon).

3. Explain: *Plan two short skits. In the first skit, the person who is responding to the situation should get upset and deliver a "you" message to the person who spoke first. Then the two of you should keep up the negative interaction for awhile. In the second skit, the person responding to the situation should try to lighten things up by using an "I" message. We'll see how these two different ways of responding affect the people involved.*

4. Give the children ten to fifteen minutes to plan and rehearse their skits. Then ask them to perform for the total group.

Discussion:

At the end of each small group's second skit, ask the children:

— *What were the effects of the "you" messages that were delivered in these skits?*
— *What were the effects of the "I" messages that were delivered in these skits?*
— *Do you think you can remember to use "I" messages in conflict situations you face in your own life?*

Don't Say "You," Say "I"

Experience Sheet

Here are two tense situations. In each one, an "I" message could be used to lighten things up. Read each situation. Draw a picture of yourself in the cartoon. Then, using an "I" message, write your response to what the other person is saying.

Situation One: You are walking down the hall. You see the biggest bullies in the school slam your friend up against a wall. Then you hear them call your friend names. You feel terrible and would like to help, but just then your friend looks at you and angrily says . . .

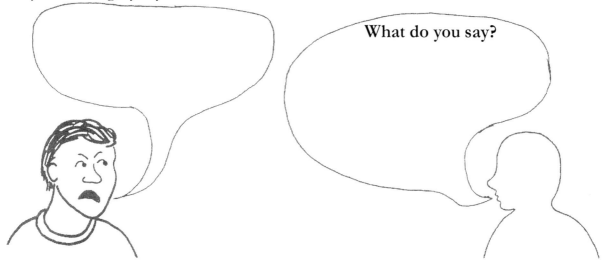

Situation Two: You borrow your older sister's CD player and a couple of CDs, but then the CD player stops working. You know you haven't done anything harmful to it, but when you give it back, she is very upset. She blames you by saying . . .

Many Ways to Manage Conflict
Drama and Discussion

What this activity teaches:

- There are many kinds of conflict.
- We can learn effective strategies for managing almost every type of conflict situation.

You will need:

A chart showing the following conflict management strategies: *1) Sharing, 2) Listening, 3) Expressing Regret, 4) Putting Off, and 5) Compromising/Negotiating.* Conflict management scenarios from the opposite page, each copied onto a separate piece of paper

Directions:

1. Give the five pieces of paper with the conflict management scenarios written on them to five children, and ask each to pair up with a partner. Explain that each pair is to act out its conflict situation, and to demonstrate the management strategy listed.

2. Give the children five to ten minutes to prepare their skits. Provide assistance, as needed.

3. Invite the actors to perform their skits. After each skit, ask the audience which strategy was demonstrated, and put a check mark beside it on the chart. Hold a brief discussion regarding each strategy and how well it works in managing conflict.

4. Repeat the entire process with different children, and ask these new actors to come up with differnet skits to demonstrate their conflict management strategies.

Conflict Management Scenarios

- Two people are arguing because they both want something. They agree to share the thing they both want. (Strategy: sharing.)

- Person A is mad at person B. Person A calms down after B listens to A respectfully. (Strategy: listening.)

- Person A is upset about something. Person B expresses understanding of A's feelings and tells A that she or he is sorry that A feels so bad. (Strategy: expressing regret.)

- Two people are already feeling irritable when they start to argue about something. They agree not to say any more now, and to settle the problem later, when they both feel better. (Strategy: putting off.)

- A and B want to have different things, but they can only have one thing at a time. They agree to have some of what A wants first; then to have some of what B wants. (Strategies: compromising/negotiating.)

Creating a Sponge Painting

Cooperative Art Activity

Tear paper

What this activity teaches:

- Each member of a group is unique and important for the functioning of the group.
- Group cooperation in a project can produce great results.

You will need:

Large pieces of butcher or chart paper; white construction paper; tempera paints poured into pie tins; sponges cut in half, or quartered.

Dip sponge into paint

Directions:

1. Tell the children that they are going to create an imaginary machine with gears, wheels, and other machine parts. They will work cooperatively in groups to complete the project, but each person's contribution will be unique.

2. Divide the children into groups of six to eight. Give each group a large piece of butcher paper, several colors of paint (with a sponge for each color), and one piece of construction paper per group member. Each person will then tear his or her piece of construction paper into the shape of a machine part such as a wheel, shaft, gear, or belt.

    Dab sponge with paint around torn paper

3. The first person will place his or her paper machine part somewhere on the large piece of butcher paper and sponge paint around the edges by dipping the sponge into one color of paint and dabbing it onto the paper. The next person will place his or her part near the first part, and sponge paint around it so that the parts are connected by paint. Repeat the process until everyone in the group has connected a part to the machine. Explaining that, although each part needs to be connected, they want to make sure that each part stands our clearly. Don't cover another part with the next one that is put on. Go around the group again until the children decide that their machine is finished.

4. As the children work, watch to see if any groups are having difficulty with the activity. Emphasize the need for group cooperation—and for acceptance of every person's contribution. After the machines are completed, have the groups name them. Hang up the machines for all to see and enjoy.

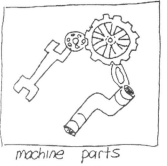

machine parts

5. While the groups are working on their sponge paintings, ask the children how they think machines are like groups of people. Compare the uniqueness of each machine part to that of each member of a group.

6. When all the groups have completed their imaginary machine, have each group explain what it has created.

Skin the Snake
Movement Activity

What this activity teaches:

• Cooperative group activities can be lots of fun.
• We can learn to work effectively in groups by playing cooperative games.

You will need:

A large grassy area, free from holes, stones, or glass—or an open space indoors, with mats.

Directions:

1. Tell the children that they are going to do a movement activity that will utilize the whole group. It is called "Skin the Snake."

2. Have the children line up, one behind another. You can use up to 25 in a line. Tell them: *Reach between your legs with your left hand, and grab the right hand of the person behind you. The person in front of you will reach back to grab your right hand. This makes a human chain. Don't let go. Now, the last person in line lies down on his back. The person in front of him backs up, straddles his body, and lies down on her back right behind him. By now, the whole group is waddling backwards. Lie down when you are last. The snake has been skinned when everyone is lying down. When the last child to lie down has touched his or her head to the ground, she or he gets up and starts waddling forward again, pulling the rest of the group up and forward until everyone is in the original chain.*

3. This activity can be turned into a relay between two large teams. The only rule is that if anyone breaks hands during any part of the process, she or he must stop and reconnect before moving again.

4. During the activity, talk about the need for everyone to cooperate in order to accomplish the task. Laughing is expected, but jeering is not allowed.

Other things to try:

Another cooperative movement activity is the "Circle Sit." Everyone stands in a circle, shoulder-to-shoulder. Then everyone turns to the right, and very gently sits down on the knees of the person behind him or her. This is very impressive when done correctly, and very funny when bungled.

The Human Pressure Machine

Movement Activity

What this activity teaches:

- Being pressured can feel like being caught in the workings of a machine.
- We can learn to "turn off" peer pressure in various ways.

You will need:

Chart paper and magic marker. An indoor or outdoor space where groups of six or more children can rehearse and perform together.

Directions:

1. Begin this activity by talking with the children about the concept of peer pressure. Ask them to help you brainstorm examples of peer pressure situations. Include incidents as harmless as pressuring a friend to eat lunch in the cafeteria, to as serious as being pressured to use drugs. Record their ideas on chart paper. (Save the list; you will need it for the next activity.)

2. Using examples from the list, analyze with the children some of the common ingredients in peer pressure situations, e.g., one person trying to sell an idea to another; persistence, bribing, bugging, threats, etc. List these ideas too.

3. Compare peer pressure to a machine that keeps doing the same thing over and over until you turn it off. Divide the children into groups of six to ten. Tell them that they are going to invent "pressure machines" that depict the idea of peer pressure through cooperative body movement.

4. Explain: *Machines use moving parts to transmit power from one place to another—like from the electrical socket in the wall to the fan belt and brushes in a vacuum cleaner. Other parts change the type, direction, or strength of the movement. Still other parts guide and control the machine. Create a machine with parts that move in different ways to produce pressure. Each person can depict a different part, by moving in a different way. Remember that the power that comes in one end must come out the other end as pressure!*

5. Give the children about fifteen minutes to "build" their machines and practice "running" them. Circulate and coach the groups. Then ask each group to demonstrate its machine. Ask the observing children to figure out how to "turn off" the machine.

Discussion:

Gather the children together and ask them:
— *How were our pressure machines alike? How were they different?*
— *In what ways were our machines like peer pressure?*
— *How can you "turn off" peer pressure?*

Other things to try:

Use the same process to build and demonstrate "Resistance Machines."

Handling the Hasslers
More Skill Practice

What this activity teaches:

- "I" messages can be used to resist peer pressure.
- A good way to resist peer pressure is to look for someone to support you.
- Intense hassling calls for strong assertive responses.

You will need:

Pencil and paper for each child. The list of peer pressure situations brainstormed for *The Human Pressure Machine* activity.

Directions:

1. Begin by reviewing the definition of an "I" message. Talk about the need to be assertive in stressful situations, and use a few examples to demonstrate how "I" messages allow a person to be assertive, without threatening or insulting others.

2. Distribute the paper and pencils. Have each child choose a partner. Refer to the list of peer pressure situations, and ask each child to choose one situation and write an "I" message response to it. Direct the pairs to share the situations they chose, and to work together to formulate both responses. Circulate and offer assistance.

3. After about ten minutes, ask each pair to join two other pairs, forming groups of six. Ask a volunteer in each group to share his or her situation and response with the group. Have the volunteer and his or her partner face the other four children, who should be standing shoulder to shoulder in a line. Announce that they are the "hasslers." The first person is a "mild hassler," and will put mild pressure on the volunteer. The second person is a "moderate hassler," the third a "strong hassler," and the fourth a "super intense hassler."

4. Explain: *Read the group your situation, and then stand in front of the "mild hassler" and deliver your assertive response. The hassler will pressure you mildly. Your partner will coach and support you, and help you send a stronger "I" message, if necessary. Proceed down the line, delivering your response to each hassler in turn, and resisting the stronger and stronger hassling. Partners, don't forget to coach and support!*

Discussion:

Allow each child to have a turn delivering his or her response. Then gather the group together and ask:

— *How did you feel when you were being hassled?*
— *Did it help to have a partner to support you?*
— *How can you get support when you are being pressured to do something you don't want to do?*

If your heart is in Social-Emotional
Learning, visit us online.

Come see us at
www.InnerchoicePublishing.com

Our web site gives you a look at all our other Social-Emotional
Learning-based books, free activities, articles, research, and
learning and teaching strategies. Every week you'll get a new
Sharing Circle topic and lesson.

INNERCHOICE Publishing
15079 Oak Chase Court
Wellington, FL 33414